Luke's Legato Historiography

Luke's Legato Historiography

*Remembering the Continuity of Salvation History
through Rhetorical Transitions*

David Brack

◈PICKWICK *Publications* · Eugene, Oregon

LUKE'S LEGATO HISTORIOGRAPHY
Remembering the Continuity of Salvation History through Rhetorical Transitions

Copyright © 2017 David Brack. All rights reserved. Except for brief quotations in critical publications or reviews, no part of this book may be reproduced in any manner without prior written permission from the publisher. Write: Permissions, Wipf and Stock Publishers, 199 W. 8th Ave., Suite 3, Eugene, OR 97401.

Pickwick Publications
An Imprint of Wipf and Stock Publishers
199 W. 8th Ave., Suite 3
Eugene, OR 97401

www.wipfandstock.com

PAPERBACK ISBN: 978-1-4982-9910-7
HARDCOVER ISBN: 978-1-4982-9912-1
EBOOK ISBN: 978-1-4982-9911-4

Cataloguing-in-Publication data:

Names: Brack, David.

Title: Luke's legato historiography : remembering the continuity of salvation history through rhetorical transitions / David Brack.

Description: Eugene, OR: Pickwick Publications, 2017 | Includes bibliographical references.

Identifiers: ISBN 978-1-4982-9910-7 (paperback) | ISBN 978-1-4982-9912-1 (hardcover) | ISBN 978-1-4982-9911-4 (ebook)

Subjects: LCSH: Bible. Luke—Criticism, interpretation, etc. | Bible. Luke—Language, style. | History—Biblical teaching. | Rhetoric in the Bible.

Classification: LCC BS2589.6.H55 B7 2017 (print) | LCC BS2589.6.H55 (ebook)

Manufactured in the U.S.A.   10/20/17

Contents

List of Tables | vii
Acknowledgments | ix
Abbreviations | xi
Introduction | xiii

Chapter 1: Methodology | 1
    Social Memory Theory | 2
    Ancient Rhetorical Arrangement | 8
    Lukan Rhetorical Transitions | 14

Chapter 2: The Socio-Historical Context of Luke-Acts | 22
    Authorship of Luke-Acts | 22
    Genre of Luke-Acts | 24
    Audience(s) of Luke-Acts | 26
    Luke's Purpose Revisited through
        New Socio-Rhetorical Lenses | 33

**Chapter 3: The Transition from John the Baptist to Jesus
(Luke 1–4)** | 42
    John the Baptist Remembered in Tradition | 43
    Lukan Remembrances of John the Baptist and Jesus | 49

**Chapter 4: The Transition from Jesus to His Disciples
(Luke 5–18)** | 63
    Jesus' Disciples Remembered in Tradition | 64
    Lukan Remembrances of Jesus and His Disciples | 66

Contents

Chapter 5: The Transition from Jesus to the Holy Spirit (Luke 24—Acts 2) | 85
    The Holy Spirit Remembered in Tradition | 85
    Lukan Remembrances of Jesus and the Holy Spirit | 89

Chapter 6: The Transition from Peter to Paul (Acts 8–15) | 102
    Paul Remembered in Tradition | 102
    Lukan Remembrances of Peter and Paul | 106

Conclusion | 121

Bibliography | 127

List of Tables

Table 1: Luke's Four Major Rhetorical Transitions | xv
Table 2: Luke's Four Major Rhetorical Transitions | 41
Table 3: Rhetorical Transition from John the Baptist to Jesus | 54
Table 4: Parallels Between the Births of John the Baptist and Jesus | 56
Table 5: Parallels Between the Public Ministries of John the Baptist and Jesus | 60
Table 6: Rhetorical Transition from Jesus to His Disciples | 68
Table 7: Rhetorical Transition from Jesus to the Holy Spirit | 90
Table 8: Rhetorical Transition from Peter to Paul | 108

Acknowledgments

MAJOR PROJECTS SUCH AS this one are accomplished only through the support of others. Throughout my academic journey, God has regularly encouraged me to persevere until the end, even though I struggled at times to understand the full implications of my PhD work. Beyond this, God has consistently surrounded me with amazing people, and I need to acknowledge them at the outset.

Academically, I have had the privilege of learning from professors who have facilitated both intellectual stimulation and spiritual conviction. To the Biblical Studies faculty at Cincinnati Christian University, I give credit for first introducing me to the depth of the biblical text. Likewise, the Biblical Studies faculty at Asbury Theological Seminary challenged me to grapple with the complexities surrounding Scripture. Specifically, I would like to thank my mentor throughout my PhD work, Dr. Ben Witherington III. Not only has he significantly shaped my understanding of the NT within the first-century culture, but he has also inspired me to creatively integrate biblical scholarship into everyday church life.

To my family, I owe everything. My parents have always believed in me as far back as I can remember. Their encouragement and support have instilled in me a confidence that runs deeper than I am even aware. My four children (Elijah, Nathaniel, Audrey, and Eleanor) have provided limitless joy in my life that fueled me during the most draining seasons. To my wife, Stefanie, a written acknowledgment is not enough. She has fought through this project alongside me every step of the way, and is the best friend I could ever want. She has made this book possible and has made me a better man since the day I met her.

Abbreviations

2TP	Second Temple Period
Adv. Pel.	*Adversus Pelagians*, Jerome
Acts Pet.	*Acts of Peter*
Ag. Ap.	*Against Apion*, Josephus
Anab.	*Anabasis*, Xenophon
Ant.	*Antiquities of the Jews*, Josephus
Ant. rom.	*Antiquitates romanae*, Dionysius of Halicarnassus
Apoc. Pet.	*Apocalypse of Peter*
1–2 Apol.	*1–2 Apology*, Justin
Ascen. Isa.	*Ascension of Isaiah*
Bibl.	*Bibliotheca*, Apollodorus
1–2 Clem.	*1–2 Clement*
De Baptismo	*On Baptism*, Tertullian
Dial.	*Dialogue with Trypho*, Justin
Dial.	*Dialogus de oritorabus*, Tacitus
HB	Hebrew Bible
Herm. Sim.	*Shepherd of Hermas, Similitude(s)*
Hermot.	*Hermontimus*, Lucian
His.	*History of the Roman Republic*, Polybius
Hist.	*How to Write History*, Lucian
Hist. ecc.	*Historia ecclesiastica*, Eusebius
Hist. rom.	*Historia romona*, Appian
Inst.	*Institutes of Oratory*, Quintilian

Abbreviations

JBap	John the Baptist
Life	*Life*, Josephus
LXX	Septuagint
Magn.	*To the Magnesians*, Ignatius
Mos.	*Life of Moses*, Philo
Mort.	*De Mortibus Persecutorum*, Lactantius
Oct.	*Octavius*, Minucius Felix
Or.	*Orations*
Peregr.	*The Passing of Peregrinus*, Lucian
Phil.	*To the Philadelphians*, Ignatius
Prot. Jas.	*Protoevangelium of James*
Rom.	*Romulus*, Plutarch
Sat.	*Satires*, Horace
Sat.	*Satires*, Juvenal
T. Ab.	*Testament of Abraham*
Vir. Ill.	*De viris illustribus*, Jerome
Vir. Illustr.	*De viris illustribus*, Aurelius Victor
Vit. Apoll.	*Vita Apollonii*, Philostratus

Introduction

MEMORY IS A PART of human nature. We cannot function without it. However, unlike the traditional view that described memory as a simple videotape-like replica of the personal past, modern studies have revealed the complex nature of remembering. We forget certain memories and remember others. We connect certain events in our minds and disconnect others. We shape our recollections of the past, and likewise they shape us. This dialectic relationship between the past and the present plays a formative role in our identities.

A primary aspect of memory involves transition periods, and the innate human desire to organize seemingly detached past recollections into a continuous, meaningful narrative.[1] This can be seen in everyday examples such as how we shape our resumes or the way we tell our life story to a new acquaintance. The act of shaping the past into a coherent whole, however, moves far beyond idiosyncratic personal nostalgia. It affects entire nations, causes wars, and inspires religious zeal.

While all humans desire to maintain an organized narrative of past events, they are not always able to do so successfully. A breach in past memories has significant implications for understanding one's present identity. Social memory theorists have demonstrated how severe identity crises can occur from a break in one's perceived mnemonic continuity. When dramatic changes literally tear us from our past, such as immigration, a hysterectomy, or losing a spouse, we experience an identity crisis. Similarly, as is painfully evident from those suffering of Alzheimer's disease or other forms of memory loss, one's present identity is severely jeopardized without a proper narrative arrangement of one's past.

---

1. Peter Berger has said that people are "congenitally compelled to impose a meaningful order upon reality" (Berger, *Invitation*, 22).

Introduction

This desire to connect memories of the past can be observed in the life of the first-century church. As the first century came to a close, the early church was struggling with their identity due to their memories of a discontinuous past. Their recollections of recent history could be described using the musical metaphor of *staccato* notes. As they reflected on this history, they remembered the origins of Christianity as full of gaps and discontinuities, leaving them to question the validity of this new Jesus movement. How did Jesus' ministry relate to 2TP Judaism? What was the relationship between John the Baptist and Jesus? What kind of transition occurred between Jesus and his followers? How did the Holy Spirit relate to Jesus? How could the controversial figure Paul have such an integral role in nascent Christianity? How could a heavily Gentile church preach about the Messiah of Israel?

In reply to their disconnected, *staccato* mental narratives, Luke has put together a cohesive, *legato* narrative, reassuring his audience of the continuity of salvation history in the midst of numerous changes in early Christianity. Luke accomplishes this bridging of past events primarily through the ancient practice of rhetorical transitions, and it is here where a combination of ancient rhetorical conventions and social memory theory can provide a fresh reading of Luke-Acts. While many scholars have noted the Lukan emphasis on the continuity of God's people,[2] no one has yet examined this theme through the combined lenses of memory theory and ancient rhetoric. Surprisingly little work has been done on the overall rhetorical arrangement of Luke's narrative in its ancient literary context. Mikeal Parsons and Martin Culy note "the lack of studies that attend to Acts from the perspective of ancient rhetorical criticism," and further state, "studies that read the narrative portions of Acts in light of ancient rhetoric ... would hold great promise in further illuminating Luke's rhetorical strategies."[3] Likewise, little to no research has utilized the blossoming modern theory of social memory in order to better understand the identity-forming power of Luke's rhetorical arrangement.[4] In this book, therefore, I will utilize a socio-rhetorical methodology, combining ancient rhetoric and memory theory to

---

2. For example, Jervell, *Luke and the People of God*. Also, Squires, *The Plan of God*.

3. Parsons and Culy, *Acts*, xxi.

4. The only monograph I have come across to do so is Baker, *Identity*. Baker demonstrates how the characters of Peter and Paul serve as prototypes of a reconciled identity for a divided Christianity. While he touches on the overlap of Petrine narratives and Pauline narratives, there is no attention given to ancient conventions of rhetorical arrangement.

Introduction

provide a fresh reading of Luke-Acts. My central proposal claims that *Luke structures his rhetorical transitions in order to facilitate his vision of salvation history as a continuous work in progress, and in the process reminds the late first-century church that there were not irreconcilable differences between the various developmental stages of early Christianity.*

I will begin with two preliminary chapters to provide the necessary background information for my study. Chapter 1 will explain the specific socio-rhetorical methodology to be utilized in proving my central proposal. Chapter 2 will explore the historical context of Luke-Acts, as I explore the plausibility of my thesis within the actual socio-historical context of Luke's listening audience(s). The remaining four chapters (chapters 3 to 6) will then survey the four major rhetorical transitions developed by Luke to highlight the continuity of salvation history at key junctures in the development of early Christianity. These four chapters will cover the following transitions:

Rhetorical Transition	Major Mnemonic Gap Luke is Bridging
Luke 1–4	John the Baptist → Jesus
Luke 5–18	Jesus → Disciples
Luke 24—Acts 2	Jesus → Holy Spirit
Acts 8–15	Peter → Paul

The four chapters will then be followed by a brief concluding chapter, summarizing my findings and suggesting some implications for future study.

1

Methodology

In order to prove my central proposal, I will implement a new socio-rhetorical methodology which uniquely blends memory theory and ancient rhetorical criticism. This methodology will be developed in the current chapter, and then in the following chapter I will examine how this methodology can provide a fresh reading of Luke-Acts within the specific socio-historical context of Luke's listening audience(s). This background work will then set the stage for the remainder of this study (chapters 3 to 6), in which I will examine the four primary rhetorical transitions developed by Luke to assist his audience(s) in fully comprehending the continuity of salvation history.

Concerning the socio-rhetorical tools to be used in this investigation, it will work well to begin with the more general universal tendency of humans to manufacture continuity between past memories in order to shape their present identity.[1] It will be observed how social memory theory provides extremely helpful language to describe the types of connections Luke develops in his historiography. This examination of social memory theory will then be followed by a more narrow look at how the ancient Greeks and Romans made these types of mental connections in their narratives. I will examine ancient historians and rhetoricians from Aristotle to Lucian, noting their tendency to shape past memories into a continuous narrative. I will then locate Luke within this ancient literary context, focusing attention on the primary rhetorical method utilized by Luke to remember the past as a continuous narrative—rhetorical transitions. It will be shown in

---

1. "Identity" can be a slippery word if not properly defined. Judith Lieu rightly notes that in antiquity, ideas of individual identity were not neatly separated from one's corporate identity as in post-Enlightenment conceptions. Here in this book, the term "identity" will refer to one's social identity, defined by Lieu as follows: "it involves ideas of boundedness, of sameness and difference, of continuity, perhaps of a degree of homogeneity, and of recognition by self and by others" (Lieu, *Christian Identity*, 12).

this chapter how both the tools of social memory theory and rhetorical criticism collectively can improve our understanding of how Luke specifically has arranged his narrative to reassure his audience of the continuity of salvation history. These two disciplines can work together to provide a rich new reading of Luke-Acts. In other words, ancient rhetoric provides the skeletal framework of the text while social memory theory places working organs within this structure and wraps it in warm skin.[2]

Social Memory Theory

To begin, therefore, I will describe some aspects of social memory theory. As the name suggests, social memory theory is essentially concerned with the social dimensions of memory, particularly with the manner that present social realities influence the ways groups envision and use the past. "Memory" refers broadly to any means by which a group attempts to preserve the past. Social memory theory rests on the premise that the act of "remembering" cannot be reduced to a simple recall of information by isolated individuals, but rather is always a complex group phenomenon. Social memory theory has developed its vocabulary and insights from a variety of disciplines that explore how humans deal with the past. Such disciplines include sociology, psychology, anthropology, neurology, linguistics, philosophy, and history.[3]

The systematic study of collective memory began with the seminal work of French sociologist Maurice Halbwachs in the 1920s (*On Collective Memory*).[4] While there are certainly precursors to the memory studies of Halbwachs, his work offers a convenient starting point regarding more recent trends in memory studies.[5] Halbwachs noted that to remember is

---

2. For a similar understanding of how sociology and rhetoric can complement one another, see Robbins, *Exploring the Texture of Texts*. I agree with a growing number of scholars that historical rhetoric studies have their limitations, and the social sciences can help augment these studies for a more comprehensive understanding of ancient texts.

3. Thatcher, *Why John Wrote a Gospel*, xiv.

4. Halbwachs, *On Collective Memory*. Halbwach's insights that every act of remembrance is inherently social were largely underappreciated until the rapid development of social memory studies in the 1980s and 1990s. During this time advances were made to his work, most notably by Jan Assmann and Barry Schwartz. Assmann, *Cultural Memory*; Assmann, "Collective Memory," 125–33; Schwartz, *Abraham Lincoln*.

5. Olick et al., *The Collective Memory Reader*, 63–173. This section of the book offers a variety of classic treatments on the topic of memory, both prior to and contemporary

Methodology

not to *retrouver*, but to *reconstruire*, aligning the image of the past with the present social realities.[6] He rejected previous "passivist" models, which viewed all memories of the past as replicative of the events themselves and the contribution of the remembering subject as primarily passive.[7] Rather, Halbwachs spoke of memory as present social *constructions* of the past, based on current needs and present preoccupations. These preoccupations will determine what is commemorated, or conversely, what is forgotten. Since the present (and its concerns and preoccupations) is ever-changing, so the memory frameworks of a community are constantly in flux.[8] Therefore, immutability in the representation of the past is never achieved, but rather as stated by Jan Assmann "the past is continually being reorganized by the constantly changing frames of reference of the ever-evolving present."[9] Or as stated by Barry Schwartz, "a charismatic epoch is not a fixed entity which imposes itself on the present; it is a continuously evolving product of social definition."[10]

This focus on tendentious shaping of the past, however, was pushed to its limits at the end of the twentieth century. Eric Hobsbawm and Terrence Ranger have popularized the phrase "invention of tradition" in contemporary dialogue.[11] They speak of tradition as mostly fabricated, either *de novo* or out of the remains of the past. Likewise, Handler and Linnekin argue that "tradition" and "pastness" are constructed completely in orientation to the present.[12] "Constructionists," such as Handler and Linnekin, argue that the sense of continuity between the past and present is fabricated by the hegemonic and ideological interests that produce the constructed past.[13] Others have adopted this rather one-sided understanding of memory.[14]

---

to Halbwachs.

6. Halbwachs, *On Collective Memory*, 40.
7. Casey, *Remembering*, 269.
8. Halbwachs, *On Collective Memory*, 114–15, 123–24, 172–73, 188–89.
9. Assmann, *Das kulturelle Gedachtnis*, 41–42.
10. Schwartz, "Social Context," 374–402.
11. Hobsbawm and Ranger, *The Invention of Tradition*, 5. In their work, they attempt to demonstrate how many European nations in the decades prior to World War I sought to firm up their legitimacy by creating a sense of historical longevity for their institutions and practices.
12. Handler and Linnekin, "Tradition," 273–90.
13. Ibid., 285–87.
14. For example, see the radical social constructionist model promoted by Schudson, *Watergate*, 54–55.

Recently, many have rightly pushed back on this extremist approach to memory, resisting the temptation to take this as an axiomatic point of departure. Research has begun to demonstrate that the past is not simply a smorgasbord from which to pick and choose in order to construct one's memories of history.[15] Rather, many have begun to recognize that the present is also influenced by the past. Yael Zerubavel rightly notes "invented tradition can be successful only as it passes as tradition."[16]

While all societies remember the past, what they remember about the past is largely determined by the traditions it has inherited. It has been stated,

> A community marks certain elements of its past as being of constitutive significance. Both identity and continuity, in fact the very survival of a community depend upon its constant revitalization of these memories. These are memories of the community's origins—'the event that marks the group's emergence as an independent social entity'—and other landmark events in its history. These memories are shaped into a community's 'master commemorative narrative'; moreover, through recitation of its master narrative a group continually reconstitutes itself as a coherent community, and as it moves forward through its history it aligns its fresh experiences with this master narrative, as well as vice versa.[17]

Therefore, in contrast to the more extreme constructionist position, it has become clearer that "both present social realities and the salient past are potent variables in these semiotic constructions constantly occurring in social memory."[18] Said another way, Olick and Levy state, "Collective

---

15. Thus, there is a reason that when most Americans are asked to list off several Presidents, they will come up with the same basic list, including George Washington and Abraham Lincoln.

16. Zerubavel, *Recovered Roots*, 232.

17. Kirk and Thatcher, *Memory*, 5. Patrick Hutton, *History*, xx, speaks of the interplay between repetition and recollection as the foundation of any consideration of the memory/history problem. He states, "Repetition concerns the presence of the past. It is the moment of memory through which we bear forward images of the past that continue to shape our present understanding in unreflective ways. One might call them habits of mind; they are the stuff of the collective memories that we associate with living traditions. Recollection concerns our present efforts to evoke the past. It is the moment of memory with which we consciously reconstruct images of the past in the selective way that suits the needs of our present situation. It is the opening between these two moments that makes historical thinking possible."

18. Kirk and Thatcher, *Memory*, 16.

memory *is* this negotiation [between past and present], rather than pure constraint by, or contemporary strategic manipulation of, the past. . . . The relationship between remembered pasts and constructed presents is one of perpetual but differentiated constraint and renegotiation over time, rather than pure strategic invention in the present or fidelity to (or inability to escape from) a monolithic legacy."[19]

Barry Schwartz, who has been one of the primary voices in this more balanced understanding of memory, has helpfully described social memory as both a "mirror" and a "lamp." As such it is a mirror that serves as a *model of* society, as well as a lamp that serves as a *model for* society. He states,

> The distinction between memory as a "model of" and "model for" society is an analytic, not empirical distinction; both aspects of it are realized in every act of remembrance. Memories must express current problems before they can program ways to deal with them. We cannot be oriented by a past in which we fail to see ourselves. On the other hand, it is memory's programmatic relevance that makes its expressive function significant: We have no reason to look for ourselves in a past that does not already orient our lives. Still, that analytic distinction is important because it underscores memory's intrinsic dualism. In its reflective (model *of*) aspect, memory is an expressive symbol—a language, as it were, for articulating present predicaments; in its second (model *for*) aspect, memory is an orienting symbol—a map that gets us through these predicaments by relating where we are to where we have been.[20]

It is in this dialectical relationship between the past and present that one begins to see the making of Luke-Acts from a fresh perspective. Luke is not simply replicating some objective version of past events, but neither is he simply tendentiously manipulating the past into whatever ideological motives he fancies. Instead, Luke has inherited a set of traditions, the same shared traditions that have formed the present identities of his listening audience(s). However, these traditions are not immutable versions of the past, like artifacts in a museum, but rather there is flexibility in the way these past traditions relate to the ever-changing present circumstances. Likewise, these traditions can be reorganized and reshaped in order to better serve the present needs of the church community.

19. Olick and Levy, "Collective Memory," 921–36.
20. Schwartz, "Memory," 908–27.

Some recent studies involving social memory have demonstrated the importance of a proper arrangement of the past for the present identity. This chapter will now focus specifically on the pioneering work of one such study by Eviatar Zerubavel, who has described the alternative ways in which humans collectively position events in their memories. In his book, *Time Maps*, he states the original nature of his study:

> While most studies of social memory basically focus on the content of what we collectively remember, my main objective here is to identify the underlying *formal* features of those recollections. Following the fundamental "structuralist" claim that meaning lies in the manner in which semiotic objects are systematically positioned in relation to one another, I believe that the social meaning of past events is essentially a function of the way they are structurally positioned in our minds vis-à-vis other events. I am therefore ultimately interested in examining the *structure* of social memory.[21]

Paul Riceour, in his popular *Time and Narrative* series, goes into much more detail concerning this "narrative emplotment" that occurs when we remember the past.[22] He observes how this mental emplotment configures events, agents, and objects into a larger whole, giving them explanatory value and thus providing identity and self-understanding. The way that humans position noncontiguous events in their minds (and in writing) is full of identity-forming power.[23] This process of connecting past events has also been described by sociologists as "framing," since we humans derive meaning from the manner in which we frame past memories.[24]

After justifying the fact that all historical narratives are socially constructed, Zerubavel moves on to describe schematic formats of narrating

---

21. Zerubavel, *Time Maps*, 7.

22. Ricoeur, *Time and Narrative*.

23. Baker, *Identity, Memory, and Narrative*, 28–29. Riceour describes the identity-forming power of narratives in a helpful threefold process. The first stage is prefiguration, and involves the pre-understanding the audience brings to the text. The second stage, configuration, refers to both the writer's construction of the text and the audience's interaction with the text. The third stage is called refiguration, and refers to the fusion of the audience's previous social memory and identity with the information presented during the configuration process.

24. Phillips, *Framing Public Memory*. Donohue et al., *Framing Matters*. Fairhurst and Sarr, *The Art of Framing*. Schwartz, *Abraham Lincoln*, 17, states, "Connecting past events to one another and to the events of the present, collective memory is part of culture's meaning-making apparatus."

the past. Using a musical metaphor, he observes there are two basic modes of envisioning the progression of time in the past: *legato* and *staccato*. He states:

> While one of them features essentially contiguous stretches of history smoothly flowing into one another like the successive musical notes that form *legato* phrases, the other tends to highlight unmistakably discontinuous breaks separating one seemingly discrete historical episode from the next, like the successive notes that form *staccato* phrases.... These two general modes of envisioning change entail two rather distinct visions of the past.[25]

These two modes of narrating the past are formed in opposite manners. While "staccato" narratives are formed by taking contiguous stretches of history and finding temporal landmarks to create gaps, "legato" narratives are formed by connecting seemingly discrete episodes in the past into a smooth flowing account. These two general modes of formatting historical narratives will be very helpful in examining what Luke is doing in his historiography. It would appear that at the end of the first century, Luke's audience was struggling with their identity as the result of developing a historical narrative of discontinuity (or a *staccato* narrative). In their social memory of the past, there existed large mental gaps separating the various progressions of salvation history. They were having a difficult time seeing the continuity between John the Baptist and Jesus, Jesus and the disciples, Jesus and the Holy Spirit, as well as Peter and Paul. Likewise, they saw major gaps between the Jerusalem-centered Israel of 2TP Judaism, and the universal Christianity of their own time. This incongruity between past events resulted in an uncertain Christian community at the end of the first century.

Luke desired to rewrite these incongruous mental constructs of the past in order to reassure his audience of the continuity of God's people. In reply to their discontinuous mental narratives, Luke has put together a cohesive "legato" narrative, highlighting the continuity of salvation history. Zerubavel moves on to describe how we as humans can construct narratives of continuity through "bridging." Resembling cinematic montage, people paste together a series of separate shots into a single film that appears seamless. "Such *mnemonic pasting* helps us mentally transform series of noncontiguous points in time into seemingly unbroken historical continua."[26]

25. Zerubavel, *Time Maps*, 34.
26. Ibids., 40–54. Zerubavel notes six primary ways in which humans try to ground

What makes Zerubavel's work so attractive for the present study is his strong desire to identify mnemonic patterns that transcend particular modern contexts. By drawing examples from a huge span of time periods as well as various cultural contexts, Zerubavel has successfully demonstrated the universal tendency of humans to create either *legato* or *staccato* narratives when constructing mental maps of past events. This allows one to look for these patterns in ancient literature. Of course, modern social theories cannot simply be "applied" to ancient texts.[27] What they can do, however, is to offer new questions concerning ancient texts, and these texts then must be thoroughly examined to see if such modern sociological constructs were present. With that in mind, it is now time to examine several ancient rhetoricians and historians, and in the process demonstrate that these legato and staccato mnemonic patterns were present in their time.[28] In what follows, it will be shown how these ancient Greek writers advocated the continuity of narratives, and these legato narratives commonly involved rhetorical transitions. This information will assist us in more precisely locating Luke's arrangement of rhetorical transitions in its ancient literary context.

Ancient Rhetorical Arrangement

The human desire to develop historical continuity is not a modern concept, but rather a universal tendency that is older than written historical narrative.[29] While the tendency to connect past memories into a coherent whole stretches back far before Greek prose, it was Greek historians and rhetoricians who first described proper arrangement of historiography. Since the time of Gorgias of Leontini in Athens in the year 427 BCE, rhetoric gained an increasing influence over the shaping of historiographical works. Also, the rhetorical school of the Athenian orator Isocrates (436–338 BCE) continued this influence. From this time on, rhetors paid increasing attention

---

mnemonic bridging in some kind of tangible reality: (1) constancy of place, (2) relics and memorabilia, (3) imitation and replication, (4) same time, (5) historical analogy, and (6) discursive continuity.

27. Burke, *History and Social Theory*. For a critique of misuse of the social sciences in historical research, see McDonald, *Historic Turn*.

28. As noted by Marguerat, "Historiography did not wait until the Enlightenment to be conscious of itself. Among the Greek and Roman historians there is open discussion about the notion of truth in history" (Marguerat, *The First Christian Historian*, 1).

29. Seters, *In Search of History*, 358.

to the stylistic shaping of historical works.[30] This section will examine these memory tendencies of ancient historians and rhetoricians in order to better understand the rhetorical shape of Luke-Acts in its ancient literary context.

One of the first Greek writers to comment on the importance of proper arrangement in ancient narrative was Aristotle. From the very first sentence of his famous *Poetics*, Aristotle states that he intends "to inquire into the structure of the plot as requisite to a good poem."[31] In listing the six different components of tragedy, Aristotle places "plot" as the first principle in the hierarchy of elements.[32] He describes "plot" as an organic whole, explaining the significance of a properly connected beginning, middle and end.[33] Aristotle continues to discuss the importance of continuity in plot, avoiding broken episodes and highlighting the logical cause and effect of the narrative. He states,

> Of all plots and actions the episodic are the worst. I call a plot 'episodic' in which the episodes or acts succeed one another without probable or necessary sequence. Bad poets compose such pieces by their own fault, good poets, to please the players; for, as they write show pieces for competition, they stretch the plot beyond its capacity, and are often forced to break the natural continuity.[34]

Writing roughly two hundred years later, Polybius demonstrates the continued emphasis on the proper arrangement of a narrative, focusing specifically on historiography. From the first paragraphs of his massive 40-volume *Histories*, Polybius speaks of the importance of a proper beginning as well as a comprehensive narrative. He states,

> One might rather confidently even declare that the beginning is not merely half of the whole, but extends all the way to the end. For how is it possible to begin something well without at the same time encompassing within one's own mind the overarching goal of the entire enterprise, nor knowing its scope nor its relation to other affairs nor the reason for the undertaking in the first place! Or again, how is it possible in any suitable fashion to draw together the events under one heading without at the same time carrying them along from their beginning and understanding from where,

---

30. Rebenich, "Historical Prose," 269–70.
31. Aristotle, *Poetics*, I.1
32. Ibid., VI.
33. Ibid., VII.
34. Ibid., IX.10.

> how, and why, the final situation of the events was brought about. Therefore we should know that beginnings do not only extend half way, but extend to the end, and both speakers and hearers [of a general history] should take the greatest pains to relate them to their whole(s).[35]

Thus, Polybius demonstrates the importance of origins when shaping a legato narrative of past events, taking several chapters to develop the historical backdrop before jumping into his history proper.[36] Polybius states that not only the beginning should be woven into the narrative, but the entire history should be interconnected in all its particulars. Bragging as the first historian to tackle a "universal history" of the Roman ascension,[37] Polybius speaks of the importance of this continuity between isolated events in history,

> He indeed who believes that by studying isolated histories he can acquire a fairly just view of history as a whole, is, as it seems to me, much in the case of one, who, after having looked at the dissevered limbs of an animal once alive and beautiful, fancies he has been as good as an eyewitness of the creature itself in all its action and grace. . . . Special histories therefore contribute very little to the knowledge of the whole and conviction of its truth. It is only indeed by study of the interconnexion of all the particulars, their resemblances and differences, that we are enabled at least to make a general survey, and thus derive both benefit and pleasure from history.[38]

Whereas for Polybius, this continuity is tied together by the goddess Fate/Fortune (I.4.1-2), Luke's story of salvation history is tied together by God himself, as has been well-documented by studies concerning the divine *dei*.[39]

---

35. Polybius, *Histories* V.32.1-5.

36. Similarly, Luke felt he needed some time initially to inscribe the story of John the Baptist and Jesus into the ancient story of Israel.

37. McGing, *Polybius' Histories*, 68. He states Ephorus was the only other to produce a universal history, and Polybius claimed it was inferior because it was before "history was an organic whole" (*Histories*, 5.33.2).

38. Polybius, *Histories* I.4.7-11.

39. Polybius also previews upcoming events and often uses the first person to tie together various events. Causation is very important for him, as he states, "I maintain the most essential part of history is the consequences of events, their concomitant circumstances and above all their causes" (ibid., III.32.6, XI.19a).

Methodology

Writing another hundred years later, two other historians speak of the importance of the proper rhetorical arrangement of one's narrative: Diodorus Siculus and Dionysius of Halicarnassus.[40] Writing in the first century BCE, Diodorus, like his predecessors, begins his universal history by highlighting the importance of continuity in his arrangement:

> And such historians have therein shown themselves to be, as it were, ministers of Divine Providence. For just as Providence, having brought the orderly arrangement of the visible stars and the natures of men together into one common relationship, continually directs their courses through all eternity, apportioning to each that which falls to it by the direction of fate, so likewise the historians, in recording the common affairs of the inhabited world as though they were those of a single state, have made of their treatises a single reckoning of past events and a common clearing-house of knowledge concerning them.[41]

Later, he again discusses the importance of the natural continuity of events.

> In all systematic historical treatises it behooves the historian to include in his books actions of states or of kings which are complete in themselves from beginning to end; for in this manner I conceive history to be most easy to remember and most intelligible to the reader. Now incomplete actions, the conclusion of which is unconnected with the beginning, interrupt the interest of the curious reader, whereas if the actions embrace a continuity of development culminating naturally, the narrative of events will achieve a well-rounded perfection.[42]

Not only does Diodorus recommend narrative continuity to other historians, but he puts it into practice in his own work, linking his various volumes through transitional techniques. Likewise, Diodorus utilizes a *kata genos* arrangement in his historiography, following in the footsteps

---

40. I tend to agree with Loveday Alexander, who states, "If you want to pursue Luke-Acts along the lines of Greek historiography, you would not want to use the great classical historians (like Thucydides and Herodotus), but the more marginal historians, closer to Luke in time, who do occasionally use preface-conventions close to those found in the Fachprosa (Dionysius of Halicarnassus, Diodorus, the ethnic historians Manetho and Josephus)" (Alexander, *Acts*, 14).

41. Diodorus Siculus, *Library of History* I.1.3. Squires talks a lot about how Luke uses divine providence as a unifying theme of his history from the creation of the world to the final judgment. Squires, *The Plan of God*, 15–36.

42. Diodorus Siculus, *Library of History* XVI.1.1–2.

of Ephorus. However, he does not simply lay an account of one ethnicity up against another, but blends the two in a way as to showcase cause and effect.[43]

Writing during the same time as Diodorus, Dionysius of Halicarnassus speaks of the importance of arrangement for proper understanding.[44] He criticizes Thucydides for the arrangement of his history by seasons, stating,

> Wishing to follow a new path, untraveled by others, [Thucydides] divided his history by summers and winters. This decision produced an outcome contrary to his expectations: the seasonal division by time periods did not lead to greater clarity but to greater difficulty in following the narrative. . . . What more do I need to say? The whole of the book is chopped up in this way, and the continuity of the narrative is destroyed. . . . A history narrative should be a flowing and uninterrupted written account, especially when it is concerned with a considerable number of events that are difficult to learn about. It is manifest that Thucydides' principle is neither right nor appropriate to the writing of history. For none of the historians who succeeded him divided his narrative by summers and winters, but all followed the well-worn paths which lead to a clarity of understanding.[45]

For Dionysius, a continuous, legato narrative provides "clarity of understanding" for his audience and in the process a firmer identity as a people. Luke, in his preface, seems to imply that he will be striving for this same type of clarity for his audience.

Writing closer to the time of Luke, Quintilian and Lucian of Samosata also offer their advice concerning the proper arrangement of historical narratives. As recently noted by Bruce Longenecker in his work dealing with "chain-link transitions," both emphasize the importance of gradual

---

43. P. J. Stylianou notes how Ephorus used rhetorical transitions to highlight cause and effect involving the Greeks and Persians. Stylianou, *Historical Commentary*, 98.

44. He considers Demosthenes the greatest orator because of his superior arrangement. See *De Thucydide* 55; cf. *De Demosthene* 51, both in Dionysius of Halicarnassus, *Critical Essays*.

45. *De Thucydide* 9 in Dionysius of Halicarnassus, *Critical Essays*. Dionysius also states that the arrangement of Herodotus was superior to Thucydides because he "did not break the continuity of the narrative" (*Epistula ad Pompeium Geminum* 3, ibid.). He continues, "Whereas Thucydides has taken a single subject and divided the whole body into many parts, Herodotus has chosen a number of subjects which are in no way alike and has made them into one harmonious whole."

rhetorical transitions to produce a seamless narrative arrangement.[46] Writing at the end of the first century CE, Quintilian states,

> History does not so much demand full, rounded rhythms as a certain continuity of motion and connexion of style. For all its *cola* are closely linked together, while the fluidity of its style gives it great variety of movement; we may compare its motion to that of men, who link hands to steady their steps, and lend each other mutual support.[47]

Similar to Quintilian's analogy of men holding hands, Lucian describes the narrative arrangement of history writing as links of a chain. He states,

> Though all parts must be independently perfected, when the first is complete the second will be brought into essential connection with it, and attached like one link of a chain to another; there must be no possibility of separating them; no mere bundle of parallel threads; the first is not simply next to the second, but part of it, their extremities intermingling.[48]

Lucian also describes the process of developing this continuity:

> As to the facts themselves, he should not assemble them at random, but only after much laborious and painstaking investigation. ... When he has collected all or most of the facts let him first make them into a series of notes, a body of material as yet with no beauty or continuity. Then, after arranging them into order, let him give it beauty and enhance it with the charms of expression, figure, and rhythm.[49]

All the above citations make it abundantly clear that a crucial component of properly constructed history writing in antiquity was to highlight continuity. The ancient historian was concerned to produce a fluid narrative for stylistic reasons, but this practice was not merely ornamental. Many of the primary sources mentioned above highlight that a good ancient historian would utilize stylistic connections to communicate the proper cause and effect relationship between various events in history. It has been demonstrated above that the patterns of legato narratives were advocated in the time period surrounding Luke's writings. Luke himself, in

---

46. Longenecker, *Rhetoric*.
47. Quintilian, *Inst.* 9.4.129.
48. Lucian, *How to Write History*, cited from Longenecker, *Rhetoric*, 12.
49. Ibid., 47–48.

his two-volume work, makes clear from his first sentence that he likewise places importance on proper arrangement, as he states "it seemed good to me ... to write to you in an orderly way, most noble Theophilus, that you may develop a firm grasp about the things you were taught" (Luke 1:1–4). Luke has meticulously connected historical events through rhetorical transitions in keeping with ancient historiographical conventions. The following section will explore Luke's use of ancient rhetorical transitions, as this is the primary technique utilized by Luke to produce a narrative of continuity for the reassurance of his first-century audience(s).

Lukan Rhetorical Transitions

As has been previously stated, Luke's primary method to develop a continuous narrative of God's saving work is found in the form of rhetorical transitions. Therefore, it will be helpful to examine the anatomy of these transition passages as well as how rhetorical transitions provide Luke a vehicle for his particular theology. While some scholars have observed Luke's use of ancient rhetorical techniques, most have simply noted the structural elements. Little to no work has been undertaken to understand the purpose and meaning behind these Lukan transitions. I will attempt to move scholarship forward through an examination of the relationship between the *structure* of rhetorical transitions and the *content* of these passages.

It will be helpful to begin by briefly exploring previous attempts by other scholars to identify and understand Lukan rhetorical transitions. The first to systematically compare Luke's use of transitions with the advice offered in ancient rhetorical handbooks is Jacques Dupont in his 1974 article, "La question du plan des Actes des Apôtres à la Lumière d'un Texte de Lucien de Samosate."[50] Here he considered Lukan transitions in light of the advice given by Lucian of Samosata (§55). In his treatment of the various transitions in Acts, however, Dupont simply observes the structural interweaving of blocks of material without examining their interpretive significance. While he recognizes the important connection between Luke and Lucian, he does not see his task as moving beyond the identification of the structural elements involved.

Since Dupont's article in the 1970's, very little has been made of these Lukan transitions until the work of Bruce Longenecker. By far, the most extensive work involving Lukan rhetorical transitions has been done by

---

50. Dupont, "La question," 220–31.

Methodology

Longenecker in his recent book, *Rhetoric at the Boundaries: The Art and Theology of New Testament Chain-Link Transitions*.[51] Here, Longenecker himself comments on the paucity of work done in this field: "Interpreters have failed to pursue issues of this sort [i.e. rhetorical transitions]."[52] He goes on to note the unrealized potential involved in the study of rhetorical transitions: ". . . they are shown to be important structural landmarks, full of interpretative potential that has remained untapped and unexplored thus far in the guild of New Testament scholarship."[53]

Longenecker examines the structural elements of various types of ancient transition techniques (bridge paragraphs, alternation, foreshadowing, etc.), but spends the majority of his time focused specifically on the "chain-link transition," as he calls it. He identifies the structural elements in this type of transition from advice given by Lucian as well as Quintilian.[54] Both Lucian and Quintilian suggest that good historiography must not simply place sections of material next to one another, but must overlap this material for a more appealing narrative. Longenecker, then proceeds to describe the structural anatomy of this "chain-link transition." It consists of the first section of a narrative (A), followed by an anticipatory section (b), which then leads to a retrospective section (a), and then finishes with the second large section of the narrative (B). Longenecker then observes how this A-b/a-B pattern gradually moves the narrative from one section to another without an abrupt interruption in its flow.[55]

While Longenecker helpfully demonstrates the anticipatory[56] and retrospective elements of the types of rhetorical transitions recommended by Lucian and Quintilian, he also rightly notes that there is some variability in how these rhetorical units were structured in antiquity. He states,

> The reader should not emerge from this theoretical discussion of chain-link interlock with the expectation that a pure pattern will be evident in every case, like the cookie-cutter that repeatedly carves the same shape out of a batch of dough. Variation and diversity characterize the examples with regard to aspects of their

---

51. Longenecker, *Rhetoric*.
52. Ibid., 1.
53. Ibid., 2.
54. Quintilian, *Inst.* 9.4.129.
55. Longenecker, *Rhetoric*, 43–44.
56. Keener, *Acts*, 1863, notes how ancient novels at times temporarily suspended the narrative for rhetorical effect.

structural pattern, their literary function, and the genre in which they appear. What unites all the examples is a perceptible conformity to the depiction of chain-link construction as mentioned by Lucian and Quintilian, with interlocking material appearing at text-unit boundaries and serving a transitional purpose.[57]

Longenecker rightly demonstrates that some chain-link transitions occur in an evenly "balanced" A-b/a-B structure, while others are "unbalanced." These more complex structures can be harder to diagram, but their structural function is clear enough.[58] For Longenecker, even while the structural elements of rhetorical transitions can be challenging to discern at times (after all, the goal of a good historian/rhetorician would be to smoothly blend these two larger units together), it is typically clear the general "centers of gravity" of these separate structural elements.[59] Longenecker rightly observes that for ancient rhetoricians the primary marker of a "chain-link" transition is *the overlap of material* at the boundary of two text units.

In the chapters that follow, therefore, I will adopt the "chain-link" structural pattern observed by Longenecker. It is important to disclose up front, however, that my structural demarcations of the primary Lukan rhetorical transitions are necessarily artificial. Due to the very essence of transition passages, they rarely have rigid demarcations separating them from other sections of the narrative. In fact, the entire Lukan project could be said to consist of transition passages, weaving seamlessly from one to the next. It is no surprise that scholarship has had so much difficulty arranging the various sections of Luke-Acts under separate subsections. The reason for this difficulty is the fact that they are using modern conventions of arrangement. However, in order to evaluate a transition passage, it will be necessary to place some limits to each passage. As George Kennedy noted in his groundbreaking work applying rhetorical criticism to the New Testament, the first step in textual analysis is the determination of the rhetorical units which are marked out as such within the text.[60] Therefore, in each chapter that follows, I will begin by noting the general structure

---

57. Longenecker, *Rhetoric*, 49.

58. Ibid., 18–19. For example, note the more complex A-b-a-b/B structure of Revelation 22:6–9, or the A-b-a/a-B structure of the transitional seam between Luke and Acts. He also considers the possibility of multiple chain-link constructions at Acts 8:1–3.

59. Ibid., 48.

60. Kennedy, *New Testament*.

Methodology

of the particular Lukan transition prior to interpreting its larger theological significance. While it will be shown that structural diversity exists even within the Lukan corpus, it will be demonstrated that Luke consistently follows the primary advice of Lucian and Quintilian *to overlap material* at key junctures in his narrative.

While these rhetorical transitions can operate on the micro-level, they tend to connect larger blocks of material on the macro-level.[61] While Longenecker notes that length has little part in defining chain-link interlock,[62] it is important to recognize that the ancients utilized more elaborate transitions than modern interpreters often recognize. For example, while many note some type of transition between Jesus' Galilean ministry (4:13—9:50) and his journey to Jerusalem (9:51—19:44), most limit this transition to merely a few verses in chapter 9, when a more detailed look reveals a much lengthier transition. Longenecker has correctly noted how transitions in oral documents were crafted in a much more extensive structure than modern interpreters recognize. These more elaborate transitions would have a significant function in an era where a listening audience would not have had the opportunity to reread a manuscript if they missed the cues of a narratival shift in direction. Paranuk notes how overlapping techniques in an oral culture can assist in the transmission of information from speaker to hearer. He states, "[Overlapping techniques were] especially effective in helping the reader [or hearer] of a text follow the writer's [or speaker's] shift in thought. . . . A speaker can help an audience follow a transition by hesitating at the point where the topic changes and hinting at the change before actually making it. . . . The effect is to slow down the transition and give listeners more opportunity to note that a change is taking place."[63] Similarly, W. Ong states, "Oral cultures need repetition, redundancy, verboseness for several reasons. First . . . spoken words fly away. A reader can pause over a point he wants to reflect on, or go back a few pages to return to it. The inscribed word is still there. The spoken word is gone. So the orator repeats himself, to help his hearers think it over.[64]

Certain difficult sections of ancient narrative, therefore, would require a slower pace for the sake of clarity. The ancient rhetorical handbooks noted

---

61. Longenecker, *Rhetoric*, 48.
62. Ibid., 46.
63. Paranuk, "Transitional Techniques," 525–48.
64. Ong, *Interfaces*, 114.

how the pace of the narration should match the pace of events.[65] Certain sections move quickly, while others require more pauses and repetition to ensure clarity of the message for the listening audience. It is my contention that Luke, following the rhetorical conventions of his day, would have slowed the pace of his narrative precisely at the junctures that needed the most clarification. Namely, these sections were the transition segments connecting various stages in the history of the early church. In the chapters that follow, therefore, I will observe more elaborate transitions than has been traditionally recognized in Lukan scholarship, since it is my contention that Luke has exercised significant effort to slow the pace at these junctures. This places more responsibility on the modern interpreter to recognize the larger transition segments of Luke's two-volume historiography. Placing unnecessarily narrow structural limits on these bridging passages greatly restricts the reader from recognizing the rhetorical artistry of Luke.

While it is crucial to examine the anatomy of Lukan rhetorical transitions within their ancient rhetorical context, it is equally important to observe how the structure of these transitions is tightly integrated with their theological significance. Longenecker has moved beyond Dupont and others by considering the interpretive significance of such transitions. He states, "It is not enough, however, simply to observe the existence of chain-link interlock in the Lukan narrative. The Lukan use of chain-link interlock leads naturally to further considerations of certain literary, theological, and historical dimensions of Acts."[66] He proceeds to make some notable contributions to the interpretive significance of these Lukan transitions, such as the unity of Luke-Acts, the historical reconstruction of Pauline chronology, and the theology of scriptural fulfillment and the trustworthiness of God.[67] These interpretive comments, however, are relatively brief and nowhere does Longenecker attempt to evaluate the significance of rhetorical transitions for the overall purpose of the entire two-volume work. In fact, due to the limited scope of his book, he does not even attempt to find any rhetorical transitions in the Gospel of Luke, but only examines Acts. The remaining chapters of this book will not just examine the interpretive significance of isolated rhetorical transitions, but will observe the collective impact of these bridging sections for the entire Lukan project. This study will demonstrate that Luke has strategically included rhetorical transitions at key

---

65. Shiner, *Proclaiming*, 93–95.
66. Longenecker, *Rhetoric*, 215.
67. Ibid., 215–52.

junctures in his narrative to highlight his overall program of establishing the continuity of salvation history. Also, Longenecker does not examine these Lukan transitions in light of the modern theory of social memory. It is here where my study develops a more robust understanding of the impact of these bridging passages on Luke's audience(s).

As I examine these Lukan rhetorical transitions, I will advance the trajectory involving Longenecker's work by exploring the proper relationship between rhetorical conventions and theological agendas. While some NT scholars have recently attempted to explore this relationship, this area of study has been surprisingly neglected.[68] Stanley Porter notes the failure in modern scholarship to recognize the relationship between a text's stylistic features and its substance:

> Many studies of style (or ornamentation) have treated the individual elements in isolation and often as merely ornamental, in other words, as individual literary features that contribute little to the substance or content of a passage, but are included only for aesthetic value. . . . But so far as the ancients were concerned, stylistic matters were not simply for decorative value but were part of the way in which substance was conveyed. . . . More must be done to treat the stylistic features, not in isolation but in terms of their coordinated use within an entire passage, or even an entire book.[69]

This book aims to accomplish just what Porter notes has been lacking in scholarship, an exploration of how Luke's rhetorical macro-structure was not simply decorative but assisted in conveying theological substance to his uncertain audience.

Crucial to this proper combination of style and substance is understanding how rhetorical transitions fit within the five basic parts of rhetoric (invention, arrangement, style, delivery, and memory) found in the taxonomy established by *Rhetorica ad Herennium* (ca. 85 BCE). Historians and rhetoricians alike would begin with the process of invention and arrangement. Malcolm Heath defines invention (ευρεσις) as "the discovery of the resources for discursive persuasion latent in any given rhetorical problem."[70] For most historians, this process would have preceded stylisti-

---

68. Rothschild is one who has recently observed the relationship between rhetorical *style* and theological *substance*, but she fails to fully communicate the complex interdependence of rhetoric and theology. Rothschild, *Luke-Acts*, 291.

69. Porter, "Theoretical Justification," 100–122.

70. Heath, "Invention," 89–120.

cally weaving sections of narrative together, and therefore, I will not dwell on this aspect of rhetoric. The process of deciding on resources naturally blends with the next aspect of rhetoric, arrangement (οικονομειν). Wilhelm Wuellner defines arrangement as "the ordering of the substance of what was accomplished in the process of ευρεσις/*inventio* for the purpose of serving the partiality/*utilitas* in the discourse's aim."[71] The arrangement of a speech or narrative was determined by internal factors (known conventions of the parts of a speech or narrative) and external factors (the driving *stasis* of the message).[72] Luke-Acts certainly shows evidence of both of these factors. Concerning "internal" factors, Luke's rhetorical arrangement was clearly affected by ancient conventions. Likewise, Luke's external motivation for the specific arrangement of his narrative was to show continuity in the various stages of salvation history.

Rhetoricians typically located rhetorical transitions within the category of *style*. In order to properly persuade an audience, Quintilian speaks of the necessity of delighting them by stylistic features that they might surrender to the case that is being made.[73] He highlights the importance of one's style to move the emotions of his audience, stating that the three primary functions of rhetoric were to inform the intellect, to move the emotions, and to delight the artistic sense.[74] In a study of the structural transitions in 1 Peter, Philip Tite states, "The transitional elements of a document are . . . elements of ancient rhetoric. That is, rhetoric, as a form of persuasive argumentation, seriously took the transitional flow of the discourse into consideration."[75]

While the ancients often spoke of a direct relationship between transitions and style, there is also much evidence to link transitions to the rhetorical categories of delivery and memory. Quintilian states, "But its Division and Composition which are important factors in memorizing what we have written, and almost uniquely important factors . . . in helping to retain what we compose mentally. The man who has got his Division

---

71. Wuellner, "Arrangement," 51–88.

72. Ibid., 52.

73. Quintilian, *Inst.* 9.4.129. Longenecker notes that Quintilian is discussing a rhetorical transition as he elaborates on the affective function of style. This suggests that transitions play an important part in communicating one's substance. Longenecker, *Rhetoric*, 4.

74. Quintilian *Inst.* 3.5.2.

75. Tite, *Compositional Transitions*, 23.

right will never be able to make mistakes in the order of his ideas."[76] Richard Burridge states, "The overall arrangement and structures noted in the Gospels, as well as the links and relationships between individual units, would help in both memory and delivery."[77] Likewise, Shiner describes the symbiotic relationship between structure and delivery: "structure would facilitate delivery since the performer could develop a particular narrative effect for each section."[78]

Unlike much of scholarship today, the chapters that follow will describe a more integrated understanding of Luke's rhetorical design and the substance involved. The use of social memory theory will serve as a convenient intersection between the *structure* of the past and the *meaning* of the past. I will demonstrate that the rhetorical transitions in Luke-Acts have been structured as such because of their stylistic value, but that Luke utilized this rhetorical opportunity to infuse these transitions with theological significance for the purpose of firming up the identity of his listening audience.

Before exploring how Luke specifically shaped his rhetorical transitions to accomplish his theological agenda in his Gospel and Acts, it will be necessary to better understand the historical context surrounding Luke-Acts. In the following chapter, therefore, I will survey the socio-historical background of Luke's listening audience(s) and observe how Luke addressed this situation in a culturally appropriate manner. This historical background information will then inform the remaining chapters, as I examine Luke's specific rhetorical arrangement throughout his two-volume historiography.

---

76. Quintilian *Inst.* 11.2.36.

77. Burridge, "The Gospels," 528.

78. Shiner, *Proclaiming*, 114. See also Isocrates's discussion of delivery, which is described as "rhythmic" in order to keep things more "pleasing" for the audience. *Or.* 5.25–27.

2

The Socio-Historical Context of Luke-Acts

THE GOAL OF THE present chapter is to develop a better understanding of the historical context of Luke and his audience(s) in order to highlight Luke's motivation for his unique rhetorical arrangement and how his work would have been received in its first-century environment. This historical background information is important in order to ground Luke's narrative in the social realities of his day, and the content here will then inform the remaining chapters in which I examine Luke's specific rhetorical arrangement throughout his two-volume historiography. I will begin by addressing questions concerning the authorship, genre, and audience of Luke-Acts. This will be followed by a detailed examination of Luke's preface, in order to better understand Luke's primary purpose for writing his two-volume historiography.

Authorship of Luke-Acts

By the author's own description in the prologue (Luke 1:1–4), it is clear that Luke had contact with eyewitnesses of the events he describes. In the well-debated "we" passages of Acts, the author narrates himself as a traveling companion of Paul.[1] This close encounter with the original events described is notable for our present study as it places the production of Luke-Acts at a crucial time when early church traditions are beginning to be preserved in a more concrete form. Thus, the assumed date for the composition of both volumes is the late first century. Witherington has noted several reasons

---

1. Witherington, *Acts*, 480–86. For a detailed look at the "we" passages as merely an ancient literary technique, see Campbell, *We Passages*. For a critique of Campbell's thesis with regard to ancient historiography, see Keener, "First-Person Claims," 9–23.

for a first-century date: First, Luke's primitive Christology and ecclesiology have no marks of the second-century work of Ignatius or other later Christian writers. Second, Luke fails to address (even indirectly) major heretical issues such as Gnosticism and Montanism. Third, Luke does not mention many Pauline elements that would have become commonplace by the second century (see 2 Peter 3:15–16). Fourth, the "we" passages and the preface suggest that Luke sees his own time as a continuation of the time when his narrative concludes.[2]

Internal clues suggest that this author was not a Palestinian Jew due to the fact he was not familiar with some significant elements of Palestinian Judaism. Keener states, "From his geographical competence and his interpretation of Judaism, it is certain that he was not a Palestinian Jew."[3] The majority of scholars agree that this author was a Gentile God-fearer, while some maintain that he was a Diaspora Jewish Christian who was heavily involved in the Hellenist mission to the Gentiles.[4] However, I agree with Mikeal Parsons that "Luke's ethnic identity is less important for interpretation than acknowledging that he situates the Christian community within the larger Jewish debate about self-identity."[5] What seems clear, considering the author's obvious knowledge of the LXX, is that this author has strong Jewish roots which predate his conversion to Christianity.

In this study, the traditional name "Luke" is used as the author of both the Third Gospel and Acts as a matter of convenience, and does not assume this person to be the physician mentioned in Colossians 4:14. However, the external clues are fairly straightforward and evidence supports the idea that Luke, Paul's traveling companion was the author of both the Third Gospel and Acts. The earliest extant manuscript of Luke-Acts (dated between CE 175 and 225) ends with the title Ευαγγελιον κατα Λουκαν. Likewise, the Muratorian Canon refers to "Luke the physician and companion of Paul" as the author of the Third Gospel and Acts. Similarly, early patristic evidence favors Luke as the author.[6]

---

2. Witherington, *Acts*, 61–62. Likewise, Keener notes several compelling reasons for a late first-century date. Keener, *Acts*, 383–401.

3. Keener, *Acts*, 404. See also Witherington, *Acts*, 53.

4. Keener, *Acts*, 404.

5. Parsons, *Acts*, 7. Green goes so far as to state, "Our ability or inability to identify the author of the Third Gospel is unimportant to its interpretation" (Green, *The Gospel*, 20).

6. Witherington, *Acts*, 51–60.

Through even a cursory reading of Luke-Acts, it becomes clear that the author has a relatively high level of Greco-Roman education. It has been widely recognized that Luke offers some of the most elevated Greek in the NT, which presents the possibility that it was his primary language.[7] This author also demonstrates an extensive knowledge of ancient rhetorical techniques and a solid understanding of conventional genre categories in antiquity.[8]

Genre of Luke-Acts

It will be proposed throughout this study that Luke is writing historiography and knows quite well the ancient conventions associated with this genre.[9] While scholars have suggested various genres for Luke-Acts,[10] the large majority still maintains that Luke was attempting some form of Greek historiography.[11] Many reasons support this conclusion (which will be observed throughout this thesis), but only a few need be mentioned here. To begin, Luke's Gospel commences by speaking of a narrative of the "things" (πραγμάτων) fulfilled among us (Luke 1:1), rather than the person of Jesus, which seemingly distances this two-volume work from the genre of ancient biography.[12] The narrative then proceeds to speak of various accounts of John the Baptist before moving on to the introduction of Jesus.[13] Also notable are the historical synchronisms mentioned in Luke's Gospel.[14] Another reason to designate Luke-Acts as a form of ancient Greek historiography is the rhetorical arrangement, which follows closely the conventions of ancient history writing.[15]

---

7. Ibid., 52.

8. Concerning Luke's rhetorical skill, see Parsons, *Acts*, 8–10.

9. For an extensive bibliography on Luke-Acts as historiography, see Green and McKeever, *Luke-Acts*.

10. Several of the most significant genre proposals are as follows: Burridge, *What Are the Gospels?*; Talbert, *Reading Luke-Acts*; Pervo, *Profit*; Sterling, *History*; Bonz, *The Past*; Alexander, *Acts*.

11. However, John Marincola rightly notes that each work involved both convention and innovation. Marincola, "Genre," 320–21.

12. Witherington, *Acts*, 13.

13. Compare with Mark 1:1–10 in which the first sentence makes clear the biographical nature of the narrative, and Jesus is mentioned much more quickly.

14. Luke 1:5; 2:1–2; 3:1–2.

15. Witherington, *Acts*, 39–51.

The Socio-Historical Context of Luke-Acts

As an ancient historian writing Greek historiography, Luke would have been well-acquainted with the proper way to construct speeches. These Lukan speeches are of notable importance for the current project because Luke often utilizes them to bind together his cohesive narrative of salvation history. It is important to examine their function within their first-century context and not by modern standards. While Thucydides certainly demonstrates that it was important to capture the heart of the speaker, historical reliability was not the primary function.[16] Eckhard Plümacher has noted several functions of the Lukan mission speeches in Acts. Finding similarities between speeches in the work of Dionysius and that of Luke, he notes that in both "it was speeches that determined the course of history. Because of their function as αιτιαι of events, such speeches were to be transmitted by the writer of history—de facto, of course, styled by the author himself and placed into the mouths of these protagonists of history."[17] He also notes, "Luke appeals to speeches delivered in the ideal early period of the church—especially speeches which were instrumental in opening the church to Gentiles—in order to resolve a basic problem of the church of his own age, namely, that of identity and legitimacy."[18] And again, he states, "For Luke, speeches—the mission speeches—played a monumental role in the process of legitimation. Because they were the decisive factors in the developing legitimation of unfolding events, Luke transmitted (i.e. shaped) them. The same applies to Dionysius."[19] Summarizing Plümacher's essay, Moessner states, "When the church was facing a crisis of legitimation and identity as it was being severed from its origins, and could no longer claim visible continuity with the founding believers of Israel, Luke carefully crafted a two-volume history, showing how events involving Jesus in the Gospel dovetail into the history of the people of God in Acts."[20]

---

16. The classic Thucydidean text in Thucydides, *History of the Peloponnesian War* 1.22.1–2 has been examined endlessly by scholars. On the topic also see McCoy, "In the Shadow," 3–31; Soards, *The Speeches*.

17. Plümacher, "The Mission Speeches," 259. For a classic treatment of Luke as historian, see also Plümacher, *Lukas*.

18. Plümacher, "The Mission Speeches," 261.

19. Ibid., 265. Plümacher, likewise, notes that the similar manner in which Luke and Dionysius utilize speeches to drive the plot forward through causality demonstrates that the genre of Luke-Acts must be historiography.

20. Moessner, *Jesus*, 364.

In accordance with ancient historiographical conventions, Luke has divided his work into two volumes of equal size.[21] This division, however, is not evidence of a disconnected narrative, but rather a necessity due to the size limitations of ancient papyrus rolls. Considering the size of Luke and Acts, it would be too unwieldy to glue both papyri into one papyrus roll, and Luke's preface makes clear that there were two rolls. Likewise, many have noted the hints in the Third Gospel that Luke intended to write a sequel.[22] While the life of Jesus is integral to the plan of God, Luke portrays his life as a part of God's larger salvation plan. While acknowledging the important questions raised by Richard Pervo, Mikeal Parsons, Andrew Gregory, and C. Kavin Rowe,[23] regarding the unity and early reception of Luke and Acts, this book will assume the authorial unity of the two-volume historiography.[24] When speaking of the unity of Luke and Acts, Witherington helpfully distinguishes between a variety of ways this term has been used: authorial, compositional, narrative, generic, theological, or thematic.[25] This book affirms the unity of Luke and Acts in all six categories.[26]

Audience(s) of Luke-Acts

In order to fully appreciate how Luke rhetorically structures his two-volume historiography, we must understand the socio-historical context of his first-century audience(s). Literary scholar Peter Rabinowitz has observed that an author "cannot write without making certain assumptions about his readers' beliefs, knowledge, and familiarity with conventions" and therefore, "we must, as we read, come to share, in some measure, the characteristics of this audience if we are to understand the text."[27]

The lack of historical information about Luke's audience(s) has often led scholars to extract information from the text about a so-called "implied

---

21. Diodorus Siculus, *Library of History* 1.29.6; 1.41.10; Josephus, *Ag. Ap.* 1.320.

22. Barrett, "The Third Gospel," 1451–66. Witherington, *Acts*, 7–8. Marshall, *Acts*, 26.

23. Parsons and Pervo, *Rethinking*. Gregory and Rowe, *Rethinking*.

24. For arguments for the unity of Luke-Acts, see Trocme, *Le "Livre des Acts."*

25. Witherington, *Acts*, 5.

26. Not completely unrelated is the debate surrounding the text of the Acts of the Apostles. It is my assumption that the Alexandrian text is much more likely to be closer to the original text of Acts, while the Western text represents a later version. See Witherington, *Acts*, 68.

27. Rabinowitz, "Truth in Fiction," 126.

audience."²⁸ This narrative-critical approach, however, has often led to an audience that seems disinterested in the historical and cultural realities of the time period. Thus, it will be important to take into consideration both narrative clues about the specific Lukan audience(s) addressed as well as the general socio-historical situation of Christian communities at the end of the first century.²⁹

First and foremost, Luke addresses his two volumes to his patron Theophilus.³⁰ While it is a helpful starting point to ask what kind of an individual this patron was, it is important to understand that Luke envisioned a larger audience for his two-volume historiography. Regarding Theophilus, Keener states, "No ancient audience would assume that the dedicatee was necessarily socially representative of Luke's ideal audience."³¹ While Theophilus undoubtedly would have read (or heard) this work upon its completion, his dissemination of Luke-Acts across his social networks would also have been expected. Alexander has noted several aspects of ancient book production that demonstrate their expected widespread circulation.³² In ancient commercial book trade there was little authorial control over copying. Regarding this wide circulation of ancient written documents, Plato states, "Once a thing is put in writing, the composition, whatever it may be drifts all over the place, getting into the hands not only of those who understand it, but equally of those who have no business with it; it doesn't know how to address the right people, and not address the wrong. And when it is ill-treated and unfairly abused it always needs its parent to come to its help, being unable to defend or help itself."³³

In ancient cultures, intellectual property rights were rarely a concern and so writers would expect their documents to have a wider readership than the initial recipient(s). Sometimes these copies were formally manufactured and sold for profit, while at other times the process took place in a less controlled environment.³⁴ What is important for our present study

28. For a caution against narrowly identifying a specific Lukan community, see Johnson, *On Finding*, 87–100.

29. Green encourages interpreters to fully observe the cultural presuppositions Luke shared with his contemporaries. Green, *The Gospel*, 12.

30. Witherington, *Acts*, 63–65.

31. Keener, *Acts*, 424.

32. Alexander, "Ancient Book Production." Also, see Gamble, *Books* and Houston, *Inside Roman Libraries*.

33. Plato, *Phaedrus* 275e in Plato, *Euthyphro*.

34. Alexander, "Ancient Book Production," 86–98.

is to note that a document like Luke-Acts would have spread well beyond Theophilus' library through a series of previously existing complex social networks. Gamble further describes this process of dissemination: "Traditionally, then, publication took place in the context of social relations between persons interested in literature, and subsequent copies of the work circulated along paths of friendship or personal acquaintance. For the most part, these networks existed before and apart from literary interests, arising partly on the basis of those factors that defined the upper class, providing it the leisure to read, partly through the complex relations of patrons and clients, and partly through the natural affinity of persons of talent and cultivated interests."[35]

The fact that Luke has dedicated his two volumes to his patron Theophilus is evidence that he envisioned a larger audience. As one ancient Greek geographical writer states to his royal patron: "I have resolved to offer you this useful compilation so as to provide through you a common service for all those who wish to pursue learning."[36] Alexander notes that the circulation of a document would likely be most widespread when there was a shared interest between the writer and his patron (precisely what we have with Luke and Theophilus).[37] All this to say that Luke dedicated his two-volumes to Theophilus in hopes that they would become enduring literature that was circulated beyond his initial locale.

While Luke could not have predicted the extended reach of his historiography, he certainly wrote his work with an intended target audience in mind.[38] Through an examination of internal clues, it is possible to ask what kind of audience would have understood and appreciated this work. From the first sentence of his work, Luke indicates that his audience is "among us," highlighting that what follows is addressed to "insiders" (Christians) and should not be viewed as some sort of apologetic to outsiders.[39] So what type of Christians did Luke address in his two-volume work? Joseph Tyson

---

35. Gamble, *Books and Readers*, 85.

36. Ps.-Scymnus *Orbis descriptio*, 5–10 in Muller, *Geographi Graeci Minores*. For more on this dedication, see Alexander, *Preface*, 57.

37. Alexander, "Ancient Book Production," 99.

38. Following the lead of Bauckham, I resist any attempt to reconstruct a hypothetical "Lukan community." Rather, it is more helpful to speak of a "target audience" for this Lukan work. See Bauckham, *The Gospels*.

39. Esler, *Community*; Walaskay, *"And so we came to Rome"*; Robbins, "Luke-Acts," 202–21.

The Socio-Historical Context of Luke-Acts

has further described the target audience of Luke which is presupposed in the text with the following significant characteristics:

1. They are well educated, basically familiar with eastern Mediterranean geography (and more familiar with the better-known provinces).
2. Luke could expect them to know only Greek (also, he uses Greek coin titles, etc., suggesting that they are probably a Diaspora audience).
3. They are attached to Judaism and know the LXX and much about Judaism, though less about some areas of it.
4. They know much about pagan religion and are put off by it.[40]

It would appear that Gentiles made up the majority of Luke's intended audience, and they had relatively strong Jewish roots.

It should also be stated that Luke's decision to include the conventions and rhetoric of Greek historiography indicate that his target audience would have been familiar with the cultural scripts and rhetorical conventions of the larger Greco-Roman world.[41] Witherington states, "To appreciate Luke-Acts's style and historical method, such a background would have been not merely helpful but in various regards necessary. One must be able to compare Luke's work not merely to and with the Hebrew Scriptures but also to the likes of Polybius and Ephorus, if not also Thucydides, as well as to writers on Greek rhetoric such as Aristotle and Isocrates."[42] The detailed rhetorical arrangement of Luke's work would have been much appreciated by its audience(s).

Regarding the geographical locale of Luke's original target audience, there have been a variety of scholarly opinions. Scholars have convincingly demonstrated through narrative clues how Luke-Acts is written from an urban standpoint.[43] However, as redaction-critical work has waned, an increasing number of scholars are reluctant to indicate specifically where this original urban center was located. Johnson states, "We are unable to determine precisely the place of Luke's writing or his readership. Ancient tradition wavers on the place of composition, and the text itself gives no

---

40. Tyson, *Images*, 35–36. Tyson concludes that the implied readers are very much like the God-fearers described in Acts. A summary of these main points appears in Keener, *Acts*, 427.

41. Parsons, *Acts*, 20.

42. Witherington, *Acts*, 65.

43. Cadbury, *Making of Luke-Acts*, 245–49. Esler, *Community*, 30. Robbins, "The Social Location," 305–32.

Luke's Legato Historiography

reliable clues."[44] Likewise, Fitzmeyer states that the provenance of Luke-Acts is "anyone's guess."[45] Plausible suggestions for the provenance of Luke-Acts have included Rome, Corinth, Ephesus, Philippi, Syrian Antioch and others.[46] This study will not attempt to locate Luke's audience(s) within a certain geographical location, since it would offer little assistance to confirm the conclusions reached in the remaining chapters. Therefore, in what follows in this section, observations will be made about the more general situation of late first-century Christianity in the larger Mediterranean basin in order to better inform the portrait of Luke's audience(s). This background information will further suggest that Luke's audience(s) had developed a staccato narrative of discontinuous events.

In the paragraphs that follow, it will be argued that there were significant reasons for the development of the many discontinuous (or staccato) narratives that existed amongst the late first-century church. Luke's late first-century target audience(s) would have certainly gone through many challenges that would have threatened the stability of their collective identity. Social memory theorists have demonstrated how severe identity crises can occur from a breach in one's perceived mnemonic continuity. Olick, Vinitzky-Seroussi, and Levy state, "Any threats to the sense of the shared past [of a nation state] by dislocation, rampant growth, or the general unmooring of cultures from their origins produced a 'memory crisis' and a redoubled search for its hidden recesses."[47] The earliest audiences of Luke's Gospel at the end of the first century would have been struggling through all of these exigencies: they had been dislocated from their Palestinian roots, they had experienced exponential growth, and their Jewish heritage had undergone a monumental cultural shift as they had transitioned to a mixed constituency of Jews and Gentiles. In addition, the identity of the church would have been challenged because of the loss of their mother church at Jerusalem.[48] As a result, the early church at the end of the first century would have assuredly struggled to maintain a connected identity due to their perceived mnemonic discontinuity of past events.

---

44. Johnson, *Luke*, 3.

45. Fitzmeyer, *The Gospel*, 57.

46. For a nice summary of the major proposals, see Keener, *Acts*, 429–32.

47. Olick and Levy, *The Collective Memory Reader*, 14.

48. James had been martyred in 62 CE and many from Jerusalem fled to various parts of Israel.

Jan Assmann speaks of a crisis of memory at approximately the forty-year threshold, the point at which it becomes clear that the eyewitnesses of the events are dying out.[49] It is at this point that a culture must turn to different forms of media to carry on the memories desired. Assmann states that writing is "an extraordinarily efficient medium of symbolic objectification."[50] This time of crisis marks when certain historical disruptions can create problems for the more organic passing of past memories. "In such cases a society is confronted with loss of connection to memory and so turns more intensively to writing as a means of stabilizing group memory, of working out connections to the past in the midst of drastically altered circumstances."[51] This appears to be what is happening for Luke's audience at the end of the first century, as the eyewitnesses have begun to die.

Another socio-historical factor that would have challenged the identity of Christ followers throughout the Mediterranean basin involves the diversity of believers at the end of the first century. In his comprehensive study on the early Christian movement in Ephesus, Paul Trebilco focuses on this diversity: "Thus, one continuing element in the life of Christians in Ephesus was conflict between Christians, and the presence of differing strands of Christian faith. A focus on admissible and inadmissible belief—and clarifying what was meant in both cases—is clearly a feature of Ephesian Christian communities."[52] Trebilco argues that the Pastoral letters and the Johannine letters address different groups of readers in the period between 80-100 CE, further demonstrating the diversity among believers around the time Luke wrote his two-volume work. While Trebilco's study focuses exclusively on churches at Ephesus, it is not a far stretch to state that this would be the general situation for urban Christians throughout the Mediterranean world.[53] What is significant for our study is that Luke's audience(s) was still attempting to work out their identity in light of the diverse interpretations of recent events. For example, one can see the diverse ways in which various NT authors attempt to establish the authority of their traditions in their Ephesian context. First and Second Timothy locates authority in the Pauline tradition and the proper transmission of

---

49. Assmann, *Das kulturelle Gedachtnis*, 218–21; Assmann, *Religion*, 53–54.
50. Assmann, *Religion*, 54.
51. Ibid.
52. Trebilco, *Early Christians*, 716.
53. Specifically, it would not be a long stretch to assume that at least a portion of the original audience(s) of Luke-Acts would have resided in Ephesus.

the Jesus tradition through sound teachers in a hierarchical leadership structure (1 Tim 1:12–20; 2 Tim 1:8–14; 2:2). In the book of Revelation, the role of prophets and revelations is highlighted as the arbiter of truth (Rev 1:1–2, 9–20; 22:7, 10, 18–19). In comparison, the Johannine letters place the authority and legitimacy of the true Jesus tradition with the indwelling presence of the Holy Spirit (1 John 2:20; 4:6).[54]

Not only were there diverse groups of believers in the late first century that would have raised questions about identity for Luke's audience(s), but there also existed at this time various strands of traditions regarding Jesus and early Christianity. Luke's audience(s) certainly did not have a fixed monolithic tradition, but rather had various oral and written traditions available to them at the end of the first century that would have resulted in some controversy. Recent scholarship has highlighted the oral performative contexts of the Gospel (and Acts) traditions, and the resultant plurality of these traditions. Rafael Rodriguez has noted that the canonical gospels represent only one instantiation of repeated oral performances.[55] Likewise, Loveday Alexander notes that in the first and second century, the remembrances (ἀπομνημονεύματα) of the early church "lend themselves to continual reconfiguration and recombination in an infinite variety of spoken and written formats."[56] However, while these oral performances involved a level of flexibility, this does not mean that the transmission of early church history was uncontrollable.[57] Rather, this elasticity would most certainly have been controlled by both eyewitness testimony and significant fixed memories shared by the church community.[58]

The variety of traditions available to Luke's original audience(s) will be explored in more detail in the chapters that follow. For now it will suffice to state that their salient past traditions had given Luke's audience(s) a foundation for their various communities, but their present situation called for a fresh arrangement of those traditions, an arrangement focused more

---

54. Tellbe, "The Prototypical Christ-believer," 123–27. Tellbe also charts the diversity between these three NT collections in the following categories: leadership structures, community metaphor, societal relations, and prototypical group member.

55. Rodriguez, *Structuring Early Christian Memory*, 84. See also Shiell, *Delivering from Memory*.

56. Alexander, "Memory and Tradition," 113–53.

57. Bailey, "Informal Controlled Oral Tradition," 34–51. Gerhardsson, *Memory and Manuscript*.

58. Bauckham, *Jesus*; and Dunn, *Christianity*.

exclusively on the continuity of salvation history.[59] The two-volume work of Luke-Acts, therefore, will be looked at as a commemorative artifact produced at the end of the first century in order to facilitate a vision of salvation history as a continuous work in progress for an audience struggling to fully understand their identity.

Luke's Purpose Revisited Through New Socio-Rhetorical Lenses

After describing my new socio-rhetorical methodology in the previous chapter and exploring the historical context surrounding Luke's two volumes in this chapter, it is now time to examine Luke's Preface from a fresh perspective. This section will take a detailed look at Luke 1:1–4 in order to further highlight Luke's purpose for compiling his particular version of early church history. When discussing the purpose(s) of Luke-Acts, it is helpful to begin with Luke's preface, which contains the only explicit comments regarding purpose given by the author in his two-volume work. Specifically, what will be argued in the remainder of this chapter is that Luke, dissatisfied with the arrangement of previous accounts, has structured his traditions into a legato narrative in order to highlight the ongoing continuity of God's salvific work for an uncertain audience with disconnected staccato memories.

My suggested purpose for Luke-Acts should not necessarily disqualify every other suggestion, but merely represents one significant reason for the unique macro-structure of this two-volume work. After all, most historians have multiple reasons for structuring their work as they do.[60] While I suggest that Luke rhetorically structures his historiography in order to respond to the discontinuous mental narratives developed in the late first-century church, this should not preclude the fact that Luke's audience(s) struggled

---

59. If one assumes that Matthew's Gospel was written around the same time as Luke's Gospel and both independent of each other, this would provide further evidence that the situation toward the end of the first century called for a more cohesive narrative arrangement. Notice how Papias states that "Matthew put the logia in an ordered arrangement" (Eusebius, *Ecclesiastical History*, 3.39.16). This, of course, assumes that Papias is referring to Matthew's Gospel here, which could present problems since Papias claims it was originally written in Hebrew.

60. Darrel Bock has listed eleven various proposals for the purpose of Luke-Acts, which all seem "credible" to him. Bock, *Luke*, 1:14.

with their identity for a variety of additional reasons (e.g. persecution, social exclusion, etc.).

In spite of Luke's attempt to carefully articulate himself in his prologue, almost every aspect of this long Greek sentence has been disputed. However, a detailed examination of Luke's prologue can assist in uncovering the general purpose(s) of the document. Before offering a fresh interpretation of these first verses of Luke's Gospel, it is necessary to address several dominant readings of the text that should be avoided moving forward.

Recently, no one has done more work with the Lukan preface than Loveday Alexander,[61] and one must take her work into account. She does some fabulous work with the Greek text; however, she wrongly attempts to uncover the genre of Luke-Acts exclusively from the preface.[62] While she draws some interesting parallels between prologues in *Fachsprosa* and Luke's Gospel, this cannot provide enough evidence to declare the genre of Luke's Gospel as scientific treatise. Witherington has rightly noted, "At most, the evidence Alexander presents may lead to the conclusion that Luke knew some scientific treatises and was influenced by the style and form of their prefaces. . . . What this evidence can*not* do is help us to characterize either Luke or Acts in regard to the matter of genre, purpose, or overall style, for clearly neither are scientific treatises . . ."[63] Likewise, Joel Green states, "Formal grammatical features cannot mask the significant discontinuity one recognizes when moving from the substance of the scientific tradition to the narrative of the Third Gospel. Nor do the affinities between Luke and the scientific tradition simply negate the identification of Luke 1:1–4 and Luke-Acts with the tradition of Greco-Roman historiography."[64] This book will maintain the traditional stance that, broadly speaking, Luke-Acts was written as a type of the large ancient category of Hellenistic historiography. This genre designation, however, relates to the entirety of the Lukan corpus and not simply the preface. In the words of David Moessner, "Luke's Gospel

---

61. Alexander, *The Preface*. See also Alexander, *Acts*.

62. Witherington states, "[W]hatever Luke may claim in these prefaces, these claims must be evaluated in light of the character of the data that follow them" (*Acts*, 3). Richard Burridge rightly observes how genre is a contract between author and reader. The beginning of the literature offers the primary cues given to the audience as to the literary genre, and this can be affirmed or redirected throughout the work. Burridge, *What Are the Gospels?*, 25–51.

63. Witherington, *Acts*, 15.

64. Green, *The Gospel*, 4.

prologue (Luke 1:1–4) has little to do with literary 'genre' and everything to do with the distinctive *scope* and *sequence* of the account that follows."[65]

There have been those who have argued that the sole purpose of the prologue is to highlight the historical accuracy of the account. This is primarily the result of the combination of the Greek words καθεξης and ακριβως. In the 1970s, W. C. van Unnik championed a strong historical purpose in Luke's preface.[66] While correct to assert that historical accuracy was important to Luke, he anachronistically pushes too far in insisting that Luke "was concerned with the 'infallibility' of the facts," that "he wants to remove doubt about the exactitude" of the events to give readers "complete certainty."[67] Similarly, Colin Hemer is adamant that the primary goal expressed in Luke's preface is "to chronicle what really happened . . . to show that the proclamation of divine events is rooted in a matter-of-fact reality which the reader can know to be true."[68] Likewise, another more recent scholar, I. Howard Marshall, states, "There is first of all a stress on the accuracy of what is to be presented."[69] And again, "We have now looked at the main features of Luke's prologue, and have seen that it indicates a concern to provide reliable history, confirming previous accounts and based on sound evidence."[70] This focus exclusively on historical reliability, however, seems to be an overreaction to German scholarship of the twentieth century.

It is not the primary purpose of Luke's prologue to highlight historical reliability. Rather, as will be shown directly below, the purpose described in this introduction is to provide fresh "meaning" and "significance" to the isolated events in Christian origins. In what follows, I will provide a new reading of Luke's preface, utilizing my new socio-rhetorical methodology. It will be demonstrated that from this first sentence, Luke sets up his two-volume project as one that will arrange a continuous narrative of past memories to provide reassurance to his audience(s).

In his preface, Luke addresses four main items: "predecessors (v. 1), sources of information (v. 2), the author's qualifications (v. 3), and his purpose in writing (v. 4)."[71] After offering a brief look at each of these, I

---

65. Moessner, "The Appeal," 84–126.
66. Unnik, "Remarks," 6–15; Unnik, "Once More," 7–26.
67. Unnik, "Remarks," 13–14.
68. Hemer, *The Book of Acts*, 85.
69. Marshall, *Luke*, 38.
70. Ibid., 41.
71. Alexander, "Which Greco-Roman Prologues," 13.

will offer a comprehensive look at Luke's overall purpose established in his preface.

The first item addressed in the preface is Luke's predecessors. Here, the attention of the "many" (πολλοί) to recent events (πραγμάτων) demonstrates the importance of these traditions. Remembering these traditions are not merely recalling distant data about past events, Luke describes the interconnectivity between past and present through the use of the term πεπληροφορημένων. Mikeal Parsons has noted how Luke has both transmitted and reshaped ancient traditions in order to stake a claim for his narrative version of the past.[72] These past memories have remained salient for Luke and his audience and have ongoing implications. The fact that Luke describes these past events as "fulfilled among us" encourages his audience to locate the upcoming two-volume story within the grand narrative of Israel's history.[73]

While Luke takes for granted that he and his audience know and accept the historical substance of these past events described in their traditions, the Lukan preface implies that his narrative arrangement is superior to previous attempts (ἀνατάξασθαι διήγησιν περὶ τῶν πεπληροφορημένων).[74] Ancient oral performances in the Mediterranean world were marked by a certain level of competition, which Aristotle terms "agonistic."[75] Alexander notes that the term ἐπεχείρησαν suggests a hint of a Lukan critique of those other versions.[76] An examination of the ways Luke uses the term επεχειρησαν in the book of Acts demonstrates that the normal Lukan usage is negative. "He [Saul] spoke and argued with the Hellenists; but they were attempting [unsuccessfully] to kill him" (Acts 9:29). Also, "Then some

---

72. Parsons, *Luke*, 53–139. He explores how Luke reshapes pagan, Jewish, and Pauline traditions.

73. Alexander, "Which Greco-Roman Prologues," 26.

74. Moessner, "The Appeal and Power of Poetics," 84. Johnson, *The Gospel*, 30. Some scholars who maintain that Luke presents no direct criticism of his predecessors are as follows: Robbins, "The Claims," 63–83; 72–74; Talbert, *Reading Luke-Acts*, 7; Nolland, *Luke*, 1:6.

75. Aristotle, *Art of Rhetoric* 3.12.1, 1413b. Other ancient rhetoricians speak of the combative nature of oral performances, such as Tacitus and Quintilian: Tacitus, *Dial.* 5–6; Quintilian, *Inst.* 10.1.30–31. For the agonistic nature of oral narrative in general, see Ong, *Orality and Literacy*, 43–45. Also, for the agonistic nature of Luke's two-volume historiography, see Rothschild, *Luke-Acts*.

76. Alexander, "Which Greco-Roman Prologues," 24–25. For a neutral sense of the Greek term, see Polybius, *His.* 2.37.4 and Josephus, *Ag. Ap.* 1.2. For a negative sense, see Josephus, *Life* 9.40.65; *Herm. Sim.* 92.6.

itinerant Jewish exorcists attempted [unsuccessfully] to use the name of the Lord over those who had evil spirits . . .'" (Acts 19:13).

It would appear that this Lukan focus on an "orderly" account was lacking in previous traditions. Both Papias and Eusebius observe that previous attempts did not make sufficiently clear connections between events.[77] Papias, bishop of Hierapolis at the turn of the second century describes the words of John the Presbyter concerning Mark's Gospel. In these words, as recorded by Eusebius, it is observed that Mark's Gospel lacks an ordered arrangement. Papias states,

> Mark became Peter's interpreter; all of whatever he remembered he wrote down with understanding—though not, to be sure, in an ordered account—of the things said or done by the Lord. For he had neither heard the Lord nor followed him, but later, as I have said, [followed] Peter. He [Peter] used to give teachings according to the needs of various situations, but not by presenting, as it were a formal account of the reports concerning the Lord, so that Mark did not make a mistake in this manner by writing down single units as he remembered them. For to one thing he committed himself: not to leave out anything of the things he had heard nor to distort anything among them.[78]

It would appear that very early in its reception, it was noticed that the Gospel of Mark lacked a certain rhetorical arrangement. John the Presbyter justifies this by stating that Mark was simply attempting to remain true to the message as he received them from Peter's teachings. It would seem logical that Luke's preface addresses this lack of proper arrangement.

Later, Eusebius speaks of the very reason for the production of Luke's work:

> Luke himself at the beginning of his own writing puts forward the reason for which he had produced his own narrative arrangement, explaining that while many others had attempted rather rashly to write a suitable narrative of the traditions of which he himself was fully certain, he felt it necessary to release us from the doubtful judgments of the others and related through his own Gospel the firm account of those things of which he had ably grasped the

---

77. It would appear that for the ancients, Mark's basic use of "and" (καὶ), "and immediately" (καὶ εὐθὺς), or "and again" (καὶ πάλιν) to transition from one section to the next would not have impressed ancient rhetoricians, who would have expected more elaborate transitions.

78. Eusebius, *Ecclesiastical History*, 3.39.14–16.

truth by virtue of his association and time with Paul and through his profitable conversations with the rest of the apostles.[79]

Without getting distracted by the debates surrounding the author's association with Paul, it is clear from this passage that Eusebius felt Luke developed a superior narrative arrangement in comparison to his predecessors.

The second item addressed in Luke's preface is his sources of information. This group includes οἱ ἀπ' ἀρχῆς αὐτόπται καὶ ὑπηρέται γενόμενοι τοῦ λόγου.[80] Alexander translates this phrase, "those with personal/firsthand experience: those who know the facts at first hand."[81] However, it is important to note that these individuals (including but not limited to the Twelve Apostles), were not simply passing on data, but their eyewitness experiences that had become intertwined with post-Easter realizations. These were the memories that were handed down (παρέδοσαν) to Luke. Parsons notes that this appeal to eyewitnesses and servants does not serve primarily to ensure historical reliability, but rather aims to persuade Luke's audience that his narrative is rhetorically complete.[82]

The third item addressed in this preface is the author's credentials. As his primary credential, Luke claims παρηκολουθηκότι ἄνωθεν πᾶσιν ἀκριβῶς. Moessner convincingly argues that παρηκολουθηκότι cannot mean "followed up," "traced," or "investigated."[83] Cadbury demonstrates that παρηκολουθέω always has the sense of staying current or abreast of something that is developing, increasing, or occurring over time.[84] Arriving at the same conclusions, Moessner examines the use of this term in various writings by Josephus, Polybius, Theophrastus, Strabo, and Apollonius of Citium.[85] Compiling the usage in antiquity, Moessner defines this term as "informed familiarity" and highlights that this term was used to showcase impeccable credentials. Moessner continues that Luke is not simply claiming to have investigated these recent events in early Christianity, but rather is claiming to have the appropriate level of familiarity with how they relate

---

79. Ibid., 3.24.14–16.

80. Some see these as two distinct groups. For example, Nolland sees these two groups fitting nicely into the two stages implied by Acts 1:8. Nolland, *Luke*, 1:8.

81. Alexander, *The Preface*, 120.

82. Parsons, *Luke*, 43.

83. Moessner, "The Appeal and Power of Poetics," 86. For a dissenting view, see Nolland, *Luke*, 1:9.

84. Cadbury, "The Knowledge," 401–20.

85. Moessner, "The Appeal and Power of Poetics," 88–97.

to the contemporary situation of his audience(s). Rather than bragging about a collection of historical facts, Luke is affirming to his audience that he has a proper understanding of the connectedness of past events and how they relate to their present situation.

A crucial word in v. 3 in order to understand Luke's purpose in writing is καθεξῆς. Scholars have noted that this does not refer to chronological sequence, but rather to a properly arranged narrative that reveals the true significance of the events. Ancient writers and historians did not value chronology as much as modern historians. The author of *Rhetorica ad Herenium* states "Neither do I agree with those who assert that the order of our narrative should always follow the actual order of events, but I have a preference for adopting the order that I consider most suitable."[86] Likewise, Theon distinguishes between unintentionally "mixing up . . . the order of events" which he claims "one must guard against" and the elementary rhetorical exercise of intentionally "changing the order of events" of which he approves.[87] Also, Plutarch's *Solon* is instructive: "As for his [Solon's] encounter with Croesus, some resolve to prove it is a forgery by means of chronology. But when a story (λόγος) is so renowned and well-attested and in possession of so many witnesses, and, to an even greater extent, appropriate to Solon's character, and is so worthy of telling and wisdom, it does not seem correct to me to reject it on the basis of chronological canons (χρονικοῖς τισι λεγομένοις κανόσιν) which myriads continue to revise even today, unable to agree on how to resolve the contradictions."[88]

In attempting to understand how Luke would define this term, Martin Völkel notes that Acts 11:4 offers the closest Lukan parallel to the use of καθεξῆς in Luke 1:3.[89] This passage in Acts presents Peter offering an "orderly" account to persuade Jewish leaders of the validity of Gentile baptism and table fellowship with them. Robert Tannehill elaborates on this observation, noting the importance of a narrative context to give meaning to isolated events. He states,

> Viewed in isolation, an event may seem to have a particular meaning, but when it is placed in a narrative context, its meaning can change. Viewed in isolation, the Jewish believers in Jerusalem saw Peter's behavior as a violation of God's law. In the narrative context

---

86. Cicero, *Rhetorica ad Herenium* 4.2.83.
87. Aelius Theon, *Progymnasmata* 86.9—87.13.
88. Plutarch, *Solon*, 27.1 in Plutarch, *Lives*.
89. Völkel, "Exegetische Erwägungen," 289–99.

which Peter supplies, the baptism of Gentiles and table fellowship with them climax a whole series of remarkable events which reveal God's will in a new way. One must understand how these actions are linked to previous events which led up to them in order to judge their significance. So Peter sets forth the matter "in order."[90]

Tannehill proceeds to describe how Luke's entire project is a similarly arranged narrative, which clarifies the movement of God in the past and unifies the whole story to give it meaning. He states, "Through revealing this sort of order in the narrative—an order which nourishes faith because it discloses a saving purpose behind events—the narrator sought to create 'assurance.'"[91]

The fourth item addressed by Luke in his preface is his purpose. The reason for offering a fresh narrative arrangement to Theophilus, et al., is ινα επιγνως περι ων κατηχηθης λογων την ασφαλειαν. The focus of this verse is the offer of a mental state of certainty or security.[92] Luke offers a fresh narrative arrangement not as "truth" versus "falsehood," but rather as having a useful and convincing quality. Luke's audience had already received certain traditions, but they were evidently still in need of assurance. Historically speaking, there was certainly much reason for needing this reassurance.[93] The church did not look much like God's people in 2TP Judaism, there were various splintered Christian communities everywhere, and mental gaps existed between recent developments in the church. Luke, therefore, sets himself to the task of providing the sort of continuity necessary to firm up the faith of his audience.

It has been demonstrated directly above that Luke desired to reshape the recent memories of the past into a coherent, legato narrative. Social memory theory highlights how all humans desire to develop a coherent narrative in order to firmly establish their present identities. It can be observed that Luke is attempting to offer this to his audience, who remembered many events in the recent past as being disconnected (which might have resulted from the disparate traditions they received). Luke will move on to rhetorically weave his narrative together in a connected manner that provides reassurance to his first-century audience(s).

---

90. Tannehill, *Narrative Unity*, 1:11–12.

91. Ibid., 1:12.

92. Johnson, *The Gospel*, 28.

93. Maddox, *The Purpose*, 210; Aune, *The New Testament*, 137; Johnson, *The Gospel*, 30.

This fresh examination of Luke's preface confirms that a primary objective of this two-volume work is to provide an orderly rhetorical arrangement that had not been accomplished satisfactorily by previous attempts. While the preface anticipates the overall scope and sequence of the work to come, only through a detailed examination of the ancient technique of rhetorical transitions throughout Luke-Acts will it be possible to see Luke weave together a connected memory of past events. In the chapters that follow, therefore, a full analysis of the various major transitions in Luke-Acts will be undertaken. It will be recognized that there are four major transitions within the Lukan corpus that address the widest gaps in the continuity of God's salvific work throughout recent history. As it will be noticed, Luke has chosen to focus on personages to highlight these larger epochal shifts. These four major transitions in Luke's historiography are as follows:

Rhetorical Transition	Major Mnemonic Gap Luke is Bridging
Luke 1–4	John the Baptist → Jesus
Luke 5–18	Jesus → The Disciples
Luke 24—Acts 2	Jesus → Holy Spirit
Acts 8–15	Peter → Paul

The following four chapters, therefore, will address these rhetorical transitions in turn. Within each chapter, a twofold approach will be implemented. First, the case will be made that Luke's audience(s) would have likely had discontinuous, staccato remembrances of nascent Christianity. Secondly, this will be followed by a detailed examination of how Luke has addressed these mental gaps through his robust legato rhetorical transitions for the purpose of establishing the continuity of salvation history and in the process firming up the identities of his original audience(s).

3

The Transition from John the Baptist to Jesus

JOHN THE BAPTIST (HENCEFORTH JBap) stands as a monumental figure in the minds of early Christians. It is clear that the early church was intensely fascinated by this individual as indicated by the amount of space dedicated to him.[1] It is, likewise, no coincidence that all four gospel accounts include JBap at or near the beginning of their narrative.[2] However, it is suggestive that Luke spends considerably more space on this ancient figure than his synoptic counterparts or John, and he also develops a sophisticated narrative interweaving of the figures of Jesus and JBap.

This chapter will explore the unique Lukan arrangement of traditions surrounding JBap compared with the arrangement of his contemporaries. This chapter will follow a two-stage process (the general two-stage organization that I will also use in the following three chapters). First, I will begin with a brief look at how JBap was viewed at the end of the first century. I will not attempt simply a historical reconstruction of JBap,[3] but rather will attempt to better understand how JBap was remembered at the end of the first century and how this would have shaped the various accounts of JBap. While certainly JBap was remembered in slightly different ways by various

---

1. JBap is mentioned about ninety times in the NT, exceeded in frequency only by Jesus, Peter, and Paul. See Wink, *John the Baptist*, 107.

2. Jeremias has noted several ways in which these two important figures are presented as similar in early Christian writings: 1) Jesus' first disciples were originally John's (John 1:35-39); 2) both preached outside; 3) both taught their disciples a particular manner of prayer to set them apart (Luke 11:1-4); 4) both called for repentance and preached about the divine judgment of Israel (Matt 3:7-10//Luke 3:7-9; Luke 13:1-9; Matt 12:41ff.; 5) both welcomed the marginalized of society (Luke 3:12-14; 7:29; Matt 21:32; Mark 2:16). Jeremias, *New Testament Theology*, 48.

3. Good historical work has been done in this field by the following: Webb, *John*; Taylor, *The Immerser*; Burke, *John*.

early church communities, I will attempt to develop a general understanding of the individual at the end of the first century. The goal here is not to "prove" that there was one specific way JBap was remembered at the end of the first century, but rather to clearly demonstrate that there was significant enough confusion regarding the relationship between JBap and Jesus in order to complicate the minds of Luke's audiences. This information will help to explain Luke's need for a fresh narrative arrangement of JBap and Jesus in Luke 1–4.

This will be followed then by a detailed examination of how Luke has shaped these various traditions in his historiography by creating an intricate rhetorical transition to persuade his audience of the seamless continuity of God's salvific work from JBap to Jesus. In the process of examining Luke 1:5—4:44, it will also become clear that Luke not only focuses on the transition from JBap to Jesus, but also focuses on the larger epochal transition between 2TP Judaism and Jesus' earthly ministry.

John the Baptist Remembered in Tradition

It will be most helpful at this point to examine the primary tradition that Luke inherited (the Markan Gospel) as well as the highly scrutinized account of JBap in Josephus.[4] However, I will also briefly examine the First and Fourth Gospels and also some remembrances about Jesus in the second century to assist in developing an idea of the general confusion surrounding the relationship between Jesus and JBap.

This survey of how JBap was remembered in the first century will begin with an examination of the canonical Gospels. This brief look at Matthew, Mark, and John will not result in a redaction critical analysis, but rather will further build the case that in the second half of the first century, uncertainty existed surrounding the relationship between JBap and Jesus. These three canonical gospels will be surveyed to gather a general idea about how JBap was remembered when they were written. While there are similarities between the various canonical gospel accounts, there are also many differences in their portrayals of JBap. John Meier states the reason for these variations:

> Right at the beginning of the ministry of Jesus stands the independent ministry of the independent Baptist, a Jewish prophet

---

4. Josephus, *Ant.*, 118.5.2.116–19.

who started his ministry before and apart from Jesus, who won great popularity and reverence apart from Jesus, who also won the reverence and submission of Jesus to his baptism of repentance for the forgiveness of sins, and who left behind a religious group that continued to exist apart from Christianity. The Baptist constituted a stone of stumbling right at the beginning of Christianity's story of Jesus, a stone too well known to be ignored or denied, a stone that each evangelist had to come to terms with as best he could.[5]

Mark's Gospel abruptly introduces JBap in a brief account (1:2–8), describing JBap's ministry of repentance and baptism, before he leaves the narrative until Mark 6:14–29. Mark describes JBap's arrest in 1:14 in order to shift the focus exclusively to Jesus, and the only other time one reads of JBap is during a Markan digression of JBap's death (6:14–29). During this Markan digression, Mark's surprisingly detailed account of JBap's death makes clear that there was certainly some confusion surrounding the identities of JBap and Jesus. As Jesus continued his public ministry in Galilee, people are claiming that "John the baptizer has been raised from the dead, and for this reason these powers are at work in him" (Mark 6:14). Herod himself claims "John, whom I beheaded, has been raised" (6:16). It is said that "Herod feared John," since JBap was "a righteous and holy man" (6:20). Certainly JBap held considerable influence, as one who was a political threat, and one who potentially had the power to come back from the dead.

Matthew's Gospel does not include any infancy material about JBap or his family, but rather focuses on the narrative of Jesus' birth.[6] JBap first appears at 3:1, and Matthew's account largely follows his Markan source. There are, however, some notable additions. As Jesus approaches JBap to be baptized, JBap attempts to prevent him, stating, "I need to be baptized by you, and yet you come to me?" (Matt 3:14). Only after Jesus convinces him, does JBap consent to baptize him. It would appear that some embarrassment existed in the early church surrounding JBap's baptism of Jesus, and Matthew attempts to highlight the proper relationship between these two individuals. Later in the Matthean narrative, JBap sends his disciples to ask Jesus if he is the one who is to come or are they to wait for another. Jesus offers proof that he is the Messiah, and moves on to describe JBap to the crowds he is with (Matt 11:15). Matthew spends considerable time clarifying to the crowds that JBap was the Elijah figure prophesied about in

---

5. Meier, *A Marginal Jew*, 2:22.
6. Likewise, the *Infancy Gospel of Thomas* does not include JBap at all.

The Transition from John the Baptist to Jesus

Isaiah. It would appear that if people did not recognize the true significance of JBap, they might struggle also to recognize the full implications of Jesus. Matthew also highlights the confusion surrounding the fasting of JBap and the feasting of Jesus (Matt 11:18–19).

The Fourth Gospel describes a different JBap from the one described in the Synoptics. Unlike the JBap of Matthew's Gospel, this JBap does not need to ask questions regarding the identity of Jesus. From his first words, he is very clear regarding his own identity and that of Jesus, the Messiah. It is the priests and Levites from Jerusalem (1:19) who need clarification about the identities of these two individuals. They ask JBap a total of seven questions regarding his own identity, seemingly uncertain as to who this man was.[7] It would appear that when the Fourth Gospel was written in the late first century, there was still a large concern regarding the identity of JBap. The Fourth Gospel moves on to have JBap testify to the events of Jesus' baptism, rather than to narrate them.[8] During JBap's decisive words concerning Jesus, he leaves no doubt to the reader that this "Lamb of God" (1:29, 36) is superior to himself, and that his sole purpose was to direct attention to this Messiah through a ministry of baptism and repentance. JBap states, "After me comes a man who ranks ahead of me because he was before me. I myself did not know him; but I came baptizing with water for this reason, that he might be revealed to Israel" (1:30–31). Since these questions surrounding the identity of JBap and Jesus needed decisive answers for the audience of the Fourth Gospel (almost unanimously dated later than the Lukan Gospel), it would stand to reason that these questions needed to be answered for the Lukan audience as well.

All three canonical gospels described above further the case that the early church continued to struggle with the proper relationship between JBap and Jesus, long after their deaths. It is notable, however, that Luke dedicates much more space to these matters than his canonical counterparts, highlighting the fact that his primary purpose in his historiography was to demonstrate the ongoing continuity of salvation history. Luke's account of JBap not only greatly exceeds the others in length, but also more intricately weaves the stories of these two individuals together. While the

---

7. "Who are you?" (1:19); "What then? Are you Elijah?" (1:21); "Are you the prophet?" (1:21); "Who are you?" (1:22); "What do you say about yourself?" (1:22); "Why then are you baptizing if you are neither the Messiah, nor Elijah, nor the prophet?" (1:25).

8. Meier, *A Marginal Jew*, 2:102.

other canonical accounts seem to place distance between JBap and Jesus, the Lukan narrative highlights their integration.

Besides the canonical gospels, it would be a mistake not to mention the evidence regarding JBap from the book of Acts. Acts 18-19 speak of followers of JBap, demonstrating that these existed well into the second half of the first century.[9] Acts 18:25-26 speaks of Apollos, who knew only the baptism of JBap until Priscilla and Aquila "explained the way of God more accurately."[10] Likewise, Paul finds some of JBap's followers in Ephesus who have not yet received the Holy Spirit in Acts 19:1-5.[11] On hearing this, Paul immediately baptized them into the name of the Lord Jesus and after placing hands on them, they received the Holy Spirit. Thus, again, Luke is indicating that a narrow understanding of JBap will result in an incomplete understanding of God's salvation history.

Outside of the canonical accounts of JBap, Josephus offers the most helpful historical information regarding the character of JBap. It will be helpful to cite the entire passage before examining certain elements of Josephus' description in order to further identify how JBap was remembered at the end of the first century.

> But to some of the Jews it seemed that Herod's army had been destroyed by God, who was exacting vengeance (most certainly justly) as satisfaction for John who was called Baptist. For Herod indeed put him to death, who was a good man and one who commanded the Jews to practice virtue and act with justice toward one another, and with piety toward God, and [so] to gather together by baptism. For [JBap's view was that] in this way baptism certainly would appear acceptable to him [i.e., God] if [they] used [it] not for seeking pardon of certain sins but purification of the body, because the soul had already been cleansed before by righteousness. And when others gather together [around JBap] (for they were also excited to the utmost by listening to [his] teachings), Herod, because he feared that his great persuasiveness with the people might lead to some kind of strife (for they seemed as if they would do everything which he counselled), thought it more preferable,

---

9. For rivalry between JBap's followers and Jesus' followers, see the following: Bultmann, *The History of the Synoptic Tradition*, 165; Painter, "Christology," 51; Hengel, *The Charismatic Leader*, 36.

10. The similarities between Acts 18:25-26 and Luke 1:3-4 indicate Luke's emphasis on a proper understanding of the relationship between JBap and Jesus.

11. It is significant that JBap's following had spread as far as Ephesus, demonstrating his great influence on sections of the Jewish population in the first century.

before anything radically innovative happened as a result of him, to execute [JBap], taking action first, rather than when the upheaval happened to perceive too late, having already fallen into trouble. Because of the suspicion of Herod, he [i.e., JBap], after being sent bound to Machaerus (the fortress mentioned before), was executed there. But the opinion of the Jews [was] that the destruction of the army happened for vengeance of him [i.e., JBap] because God willed to afflict Herod.[12]

What seems to stand out here is the sway that JBap had with the people. Clearly he was a man of persuasiveness and this would have brought forth many followers. It is also notable that while the Gospel writers claim JBap's moral integrity as the sole reason for his execution, Josephus notes the political ramifications for Herod as the cause for death.[13] These accounts are not in conflict, however, but simply emphasize the large impact of JBap's prophetic message, which touched on the social, moral, ethical, and political fabric of his society. The geographical location of JBap's ministry (in the Transjordan wilderness) would have implied, either explicitly or implicitly, political subversion, and Herod Antipas felt threatened.[14] Anyone remembered as having the potential for political upheaval would have naturally been misunderstood at times. Also, such a significant individual would seem to have quite the following, both in his own time and after his death as well.

Also notable for our study are the words relating JBap and Jesus in the Gospel of the Nazareans in the early second century:

> Behold the mother of the Lord and his brethren said to him: John the Baptist baptizes unto the remission of sins, let us go and be baptized by him. But he said to them: Wherein have I sinned that I should go and be baptized by him? Unless what I have said is ignorance (a sin of ignorance).[15]

What is clear from this passage is that Jesus' baptism by JBap remained a source of difficulty for some in the church into the second century. This

---

12. Josephus, *Ant.* 118.116–19. For a defense of the authenticity of this passage see Webb, *John*, 31–41. Also, see Meier, *A Marginal Jew*, 2:19–22 and Hoehner, *Herod Antipas*, 136–46.

13. Dapaah, *The Relationship*, 49.

14. Ibid.

15. The fragment, from *Gospel of the Nazareans* 2, was originally derived from Jerome, *Adv. Pel.* 3.2. For an introduction to the *Gospel of the Nazareans* and a full text, see Schneemelcher and Wilson, *New Testament Apocrypha*, 1.139–53.

passage strongly implies that Jesus' baptism by JBap suggested inferiority, and it also potentially placed Jesus' sinlessness in doubt.[16] At least some confusion surrounding the enigmatic figure JBap survived into the second century.

Another second-century source that reveals the manner in which the church remembered JBap is *The Protoevangelium of James*. While this source is not helpful in reconstructing a portrait of the "historical" JBap since it relies heavily on the Infancy Narratives of Luke and Matthew, it can provide information regarding how those in the mid-second century remembered the relationship between JBap and Jesus. While both this ancient work and the Gospel of Luke seem to address some similar topics, their narratives are shaped differently. In *Prot. Jas.*, the narrative begins with Jesus' lineage rather than that of JBap, apparently to highlight the superiority of Jesus over JBap. The author of *Prot. Jas.* connects Jesus to the OT exclusively through the lineage of his mother, Mary. The author spends some time initially connecting Mary's parents, Ioacim and Anna, to the Twelve Tribes of Israel (I.1–2). When JBap's family is mentioned, the primary focus is not on JBap, but rather his parents, Zechariah and Elizabeth. JBap maintains a rather passive role, and he is not spoken of as a forerunner to Jesus. He only leaps in his mother's womb when Mary visits Elizabeth (XII.2), and he is miraculously protected from Herod (XII.3). This account seems more focused on the parents of JBap and Jesus than on the children themselves. To the contrary, the Gospel of Luke attempts to focus on interweaving the lives of JBap and Jesus from very early on.

How, then, was JBap remembered at the end of the first century? From the above sources, it remains clear that toward the end of the first century, much confusion existed regarding the relationship between JBap and Jesus. Meier states that the early church's interpretation of JBap "aims at neutralizing the Baptist's independence to make him safe for Christianity."[17] Likewise, in a classic treatment of JBap, Walter Wink states the traditional stance on the inclusion of JBap in the Gospel accounts: "The reason which scholars have generally advanced is that the early church found itself in continuing competition with John's disciples, and that as an evangelistic stratagem the church absorbed John into the Gospel message, making John a witness against his own disciples to the messiahship of Jesus."[18] However,

---

16. Webb, *John*, 83.
17. Meier, "John the Baptist," 384.
18. Wink, *John*, xi.

Wink does observes that this is only a partial reason for the inclusion of the Baptist material in the Gospels and rightly notes that this remembered figure also has been included in the traditions for more complex reasons than apologetic.[19] Wink states the best way to understand the significance of JBap for his original hearers is to ask "What is the role of John the Baptist in God's redemptive purpose?"[20] This seems to be the question that Luke's audience is struggling to answer at the end of the first century. Luke, aware of the many disconnected, staccato traditions available to his audiences, will strategically arrange these pieces of history into a legato narrative in order to firm up the identity of the early church.

Lukan Remembrances of John the Baptist and Jesus

Having already examined the ways the first- and second-century church struggled to remember the continuity between JBap and Jesus, this chapter will now move to explore how Luke has (re)shaped various traditions to highlight this continuity. Many Lukan scholars have noted the parallels between the birth stories of JBap and Jesus,[21] but none have yet identified this section as an elaborate rhetorical transition to develop continuity between past memories. This chapter, therefore, will demonstrate that Luke has developed a sophisticated rhetorical transition in Luke 1:5-4:44 in order to weave together the lives of JBap (and the 2TP Judaism which he represented) and Jesus, demonstrating the continuity of salvation history in the process.

It is not surprising that commentators have often struggled to neatly divide the literary structure of the early chapters of Luke, since Luke never intended for a simple demarcation in the first place. There have been many who have attempted to create an artificial division between JBap and Jesus in the Lukan narrative. One reason for this is the source-critical work that has ostracized the Infancy Narratives from the "narrative proper." There have been various suggestions regarding sources behind the Infancy Narratives. Raymond Brown notes three primary sources that have been

---

19. Some have argued that Luke has utilized the Hellenistic practice of synkrisis here. See Plutarch's *Lives*. Also see Focke, "Synkrisis," 327-68; and Fearghail, *The Introduction*, 33-36.

20. Wink, *John*, xii.

21. Nolland, *Luke*, 1:24. Marshall, *The Gospel*, 45. Green, *The Gospel*, 51.

proposed: 1) a special source for canticles; 2) sources for one or more units in chapter 2; and 3) sources for the JBap and Jesus stories of ch. 1.[22] Luke's careful interweaving of sources into his narrative make these pre-Lukan traditions difficult to discern. While it is likely that Luke began with certain traditions surrounding the births of JBap and Jesus, this chapter will focus largely on the final form of the narrative and how Luke has rhetorically arranged the overall narrative (which includes traditions and his own unique literary creations as well).[23]

One reason for the artificial separation of JBap and Jesus in Lukan scholarship has been the work of Hanz Conzelmann. Many have been influenced by Conzelmann, who utilized a redaction-critical methodology to observe a division between JBap and Jesus. Utilizing Luke 16:16, he claims that Luke's portrait of salvation history includes two distinct epochs between JBap and Jesus.[24] Conzelmann states, "John has a clearly defined function in the centre of the story of salvation. As it is his ministry rather than his person that serves as a preparation for Jesus, he is subordinate to the work of Jesus in the same way as is the whole epoch of the Law."[25] In this way, JBap remains firmly planted exclusively in the long line of OT prophets, distinct from the realized eschatology of Jesus. With such a rigid schema, it is not surprising that Conzelmann found no place for the Infancy Narratives in Luke's overall theological agenda.[26]

There have been many who have rightly pushed back against the artificial divisions erected by source- and redaction-critical work, such as that offered by Conzelmann. Speaking of the internal coherence of Luke 1:5—4:15, Talbert argues that this entire section anticipates Jesus' public

---

22. Brown, *The Birth*, 244, 349.

23. Taking seriously the author's comments in Luke 1:1–4, it is likely that Luke would have collected some of these traditions from eyewitness interviews with members of Jesus' family.

24. Most of the controversy surrounding the difficult passage of Luke 16:16 concerns the word μεχρι and the phrase απο τοτε. NT usage demonstrates that these phrases could take either an inclusive or exclusive interpretation, so this passage must not be determinative for any particular schema of salvation history. The NT usages of the phrase are: Matt 11:23; 28:15; Mark 13:30; Luke 16:16; Acts 10:30; 20:7; Rom 5:14; 15:19; Gal 4:19; Eph 4:13; Phil 2:8; 2:30; 1 Tim 6:14; 2 Tim 2:9; Heb 3:14; 9:10; 12:4.

25. Conzelmann, *The Theology of St. Luke*, 24.

26. Ibid., 172. For rebuttal, see Minear, "Luke's Use of the Birth Stories," 111–30. Also, see Oliver, "The Lucan Birth Stories," 202–26. More recently, see Tyson, "The Birth Narratives," 103–20.

destiny.²⁷ Likewise, Joel Green states, "Whereas 1:5—2:52 establishes the *possibility* of Jesus' mission as Son of God, 3:1—4:13 establishes its *probability* before that ministry actually commences with Luke 4:14."²⁸ Green moves on to assert that "Luke 1–2 is incomplete in itself and utterly dependent on the narrative that follows."²⁹

Many recent scholars have begun to recognize JBap as an integral bridge figure who stands between the OT and Jesus. For example, Marshall states, "It is better to see him [JBap] as a bridge figure, belonging to both eras; his coming marks both the end of the old and the beginning of the new. His function is preparatory, but is essentially part of the new era."³⁰ In light of the wide-ranging impact of JBap in Luke's own day (see Acts 13:24–25; 18:25; 19:1–4), it is not surprising that Luke decided to spend considerable time transitioning from JBap to Jesus, and showing Jesus to be superior in the process.³¹ The transition between JBap and Jesus, however, has additional significance in that it signals the transition from the more traditional Jewish aspects of 2TP Judaism to the teaching and ministry of Jesus. Raymond Brown notes the role of OT allusions in weaving together the past and present, "The common instinct to draw so heavily upon the Scriptures suggests that for each evangelist [Luke and Matthew] the infancy narrative was to supply a transition from the OT to the Gospel—the christological preaching of the Church presented in the imagery of Israel."³² JBap serves as a sort of convenient point of intersection, linking God's work in Jewish history and God's work in Jesus. To an audience struggling to fully comprehend their identity, this is an important first transition in the Lukan corpus.

While recent scholarship is correct to note the connectedness of these opening chapters in Luke's Gospel, they have failed to miss the place of these chapters in Luke's larger rhetorical structure. I propose that these early narratives are integrally woven together to show the continuity of God's salvation for an audience struggling to put the historical pieces together. The remainder of this chapter, therefore, will examine Luke 1:5—4:44 in detail, noting the purposeful rhetorical interweaving along the way. In the

---

27. Talbert, "Prophecies," 129–41.
28. Green, *The Gospel*, 49.
29. Ibid.
30. Marshall, *The Gospel*, 132.
31. Green, *The Gospel*, 51.
32. Brown, *The Birth*, 37.

process, it will also be noted how social memory theory can aid us in understanding Luke's purposes here.

As this is the very first Lukan rhetorical transition in his two-volume work, it carries significant meaning since it introduces his entire narrative.[33] Beginnings in any culture have significant meaning. Zerubavel states, "*Origins* help articulate identities, and where communities locate their beginnings tells us quite a lot about how they perceive themselves."[34] The significance of beginnings can be observed in ancient cultures as well as modern ones. This is particularly noticeable in ancient literature of oral cultures.[35] It is helpful here to note the similarities between Luke's beginning and the beginning of Polybius' *Histories*. In this massive 40 volume historiography of the Roman Empire, Polybius elaborates on the proper beginning for his historiography.[36] He discusses the chain of endless causes for historical events, but realizes that a historian must begin at some point, and the best place is to find common ground with the audience that everyone can agree on. Therefore, prior to the real focus on his "history proper" in book 3, Polybius spends two books discussing what has led to this point in human history. Likewise, Luke spends roughly two "preliminary" chapters preparing for his history proper. After completing these preliminary books, Polybius states, "I have now given a continuous account suitable to this preliminary plan of my book . . ."[37]

One can see a similar purpose in Luke's opening chapters, as he seeks to utilize the character JBap in order to develop a continuous chain connecting God's salvific work in past Judaism to the saving work of Jesus. Zerubavel speaks of the use of ancestry and descent in order to bridge the past and present.[38] This can be seen in modern society in a variety of ways. The most obvious connection is biological, as families speak of themselves as having the same "blood" as previous generations. Genealogical linkages

---

33. Johnson notes that since Luke's primary source (Mark's Gospel) does not include an infancy narrative, Luke was "largely free to shape the narrative according to his own perceptions." Johnson moves on to state, "These chapters [Luke 1–2] are, therefore, like Acts, of particular importance in showing the reader how Luke intended his story to be understood" (Johnson, *The Gospel*, 34).

34. Zerubavel, *Time Maps*, 101.

35. For one who views Luke-Acts as "a narrative of beginnings," see Sterling, *Historiography*.

36. See *Histories* 5.32.1–5 for further thoughts by Polybius about a proper beginning.

37. Polybius, *Histories* 2.37.1–4.

38. Zerubavel, *Time Maps*, 55–81.

The Transition from John the Baptist to Jesus

are one of the most common ways people remember their continuity with the past, and a loss of this continuity can lead to identity crisis.[39] But these links to the past can be artificially developed as well. Many organizations use past members (such as college alumni) to recruit future ones. Likewise, the U.S. presidents are linked in a chain, in which Barak Obama is the forty-fourth link and George Washington is the first.[40] Or take the Papacy succession, for example. While there are periods (such as from 304–308 and 638–640) when there was no Pope, this is remembered in such a way that there is a successive link. Zerubavel states, "Having a common past also entails some general sense of sharing a common present."[41] It will be observed how Luke has shaped the narratives of JBap and Jesus in order to highlight both genealogical links and artificial links to Israel's past.

It should not be surprising that Luke adds a genealogy where Mark has none. It is also notable that Luke has arranged his genealogy differently than Matthew's, showing continuity from Jesus all the way back to Adam (and ultimately to God himself). This demonstrates a type of continuity between all humanity, whereas Matthew's genealogy demonstrates a continuity with the Jewish ethnicity only (since it begins with Abraham). These types of differences highlight the difference in genre between Luke-Acts (historiography) and the other canonical gospels (*bioi*).

The interweaving of the stories of JBap and Jesus have been widely recognized in recent Lukan scholarship. What has been lacking, however, is both the rhetorical exigency motivating such an arrangement and the rhetorical effect of this particular narrative transition. Likewise, scholars have yet to incorporate the insights of social memory to better understand intended mnemonic continuity at this juncture in Luke's narrative. While many scholars treat Luke 1–2 separate from Luke 3–4, I will propose that Luke has purposefully arranged all of Luke 1:5—4:44 into an elaborate transition, which methodically alternates from JBap to Jesus throughout. Since this is a gradual oral transition, it is not surprising that a myriad of

---

39. Ibid., 63. Just look at the stigma of illegitimacy as well as the identity crisis that follows from finding out one is adopted. Likewise, African Americans often feel disconnected from their beginnings, and the greatest punishment in many cultures is having one's name struck from their family's genealogical records.

40. One might note how Luke immediately begins his narrative by describing a "priest" in the line of priests (Abijah) and his wife Elizabeth was from the daughters of Aaron. Luke also links Zechariah and Elizabeth to the land of Judea, with its rich heritage.

41. Zerubavel, *Time Maps*, 63.

proposals have been suggested concerning the literary boundaries of this first major section of Luke's Gospel.[42] None of these proposals, however, have considered Luke 1–4 as an extended rhetorical transition. The following rhetorical arrangement can be observed:

A	Announcement of the Birth of JBap	1:5–25
b	Announcement of the Birth of Jesus	1:26–56
a	Birth and Growth of JBap	1:57–80
b	Birth and Growth of Jesus	2:1–52
a	Public Ministry of JBap Commences	3:1–20
B	Public Ministry of Jesus Commences	3:21—4:44

This first transition in the Lukan corpus evidences the most unique structure in his historiographical work. The A-b-a-b/a-B arrangement extends the more typical A-b/a-B "chain-link" structure to include two anticipatory sections ("b"; 1:26–56 and 2:1–52) and two retrospective sections ("a"; 1:57–80 and 3:1–20). In this way, Luke's rhetorical design resembles three links of a chain instead of the more typical two links in the rest of his transition sections. Perhaps this uniquely extended chain-link transition is indicative of the high level of disconnect between JBap and Jesus in the memories of Luke's listening audience. Luke offers his audience plenty of time to anticipate the greater ministry of Jesus which would follow that of JBap, presenting them an opportunity to pause on the multiple retrospective elements which remind them that Jesus' ministry is intimately connected to that of JBap's which preceded him. It becomes increasingly clear, therefore, that Luke's first audience(s) would have spent time in these lengthy opening chapters reevaluating the continuity between JBap and Jesus.

Paranuk and Ong note how these rhetorical "pauses" at transitions in the narrative allow the audience to follow along.[43] In his oral culture, Luke's lengthy transitional arrangement from JBap to Jesus offered his audience some time to reflect on the connectedness of salvation history. Luke pairs the life stages of these two individuals in a way that prepares his hearers for the movement of salvation history from one to the other. The anticipatory elements of this rhetorical transition offer the audience an opportunity to better synthesize the place of these two personages in history. Likewise the retrospective passages of JBap in this Lukan transition ground the ministry

---

42. For a variety of commonly made proposals, see Fearghail, *The Introduction*, 1–7. For the classical division of the birth narratives, see Brown, *The Birth*, 250.

43. Paranuk, "Transitional Techniques," 546; Ong, *Interfaces*, 114.

of Jesus in the 2TP Judaism which preceded him (represented by JBap). In what follows, I will examine the various sections of this particular Lukan rhetorical transition, noting how Luke stylistically persuades his first-century audience of the continuity between JBap and Jesus, and in the process demonstrates the superiority of the latter. It will be shown how Luke navigates the audience from the central character of JBap (1:5–25) to the central character of Jesus (3:21—4:44) through this elaborate transition section.

Announcement of the Birth of JBap (1:5–25)

In the Birth Narratives at the beginning of Luke's two-volume historiography, he has carefully begun his story in the language of ancient Judaism. While he describes the more recent events of the births of JBap and Jesus, they are described in the language of the Greek Bible (LXX). Johnson rightly notes how the Semitisms in this section should not lead one to suspect Hebrew or Aramaic sources behind every Semitism, but rather that Luke was skillfully imitating biblical language in his narrative artistry.[44] Johnson states, "So skillful is he that the reader is plunged into the world of Ruth, the Judges, and Samuel. Imaginatively, then, the reader begins in the biblical world of Temple and Torah, and instinctively feels, 'this is part of *our* story.'"[45]

It should come as no surprise, then, that Luke's narrative begins with a Temple scene, designed to assist his audience in viewing themselves as part of a larger story. From the outset of the infancy narrative, Luke stresses how "both geographically and theologically the focus of Christianity passed from Jerusalem of the Jews to Rome of the Gentiles."[46] Luke purposefully frames his Gospel of Jesus in scenes involving the Jerusalem Temple (1:8 and 24:53), and even uses a minor Temple *inclusio* to frame the infancy narratives (1:8 and 2:41). Later in this narrative, Jesus will spend half of his ministry on a journey toward the Jerusalem Temple, and it is notable that only Luke mentions no Galilean post-resurrection appearances of Jesus, but rather they take place in the Jerusalem area.[47] This is a thoroughly Jewish beginning which purposefully ties ancient Jewish roots with Luke's primarily Gentile audience. Developing continuity

---

44. Johnson, *The Gospel*, 34.
45. Ibid., 34–35.
46. Brown, *The Birth*, 237.
47. Ibid.

between ancient Judaism and his contemporary Christianity remains a primary theological agenda for Luke.

Announcement of the Birth of Jesus (1:26–56)

As Luke begins to narrate Jesus' birth announcement, the audience immediately notes a connection to JBap's birth announcement that immediately preceded. The angel Gabriel is back again, highlighting that God is orchestrating another event in salvation history that will have continuity with the prophecy just given to Zechariah. These two children will be inseparably linked.

As Luke continues to narrate the various aspects surrounding the births of JBap and Jesus, the parallels are numerous. Fearghail notes the following general parallels:[48]

Events During the Birth Narratives	JBap's Birth	Jesus' Birth
Announcement of Conception[49]	1:5–25	1:26–38
Visitation	1:39–56	1:39–56
Birth	1:57–58	2:1–20
Circumcision and Naming	1:59–66	2:21
Praise and Prophecy	1:67–79	2:22–39
Growth; Life Prior to Public Ministry	1:80	2:40–52

Fearghail moves on to describe the various detailed similarities in the narratives surrounding these two births. In the announcement narratives, these parallels include the following: the angelophanies; the birth oracles with the role and identity of each described; significant linguistic links, such as the use of ταρασσω and διαταρασσω to describe the reactions of Zachariah and Mary; septuagintal reminiscences (i.e. those recalling the conception of Isaac in Gen 18:11, 14; cf. Luke 1:7, 18, 37).[50] It becomes clear throughout the Lukan birth narratives that God has woven the lives of these two central characters together.

The stories of JBap (and his family) and Jesus (and his family) link most explicitly as Mary and Elizabeth meet in Luke 1:39–56. It is during

---

48. Fearghail, *The Introduction*, 16.

49. For more detailed parallelism between the two announcements, see Keener, *Acts*, 557.

50. Fearghail, *The Introduction*, 16. See also Brown, *The Birth*, 297–300.

this narrative section that Luke explicitly draws out the familial relationship (1:36) between Elizabeth and Mary (and consequently John and Jesus), whereas the other canonical Gospel accounts do not. Based on the importance of kinship in antiquity, this is further evidence that Luke desires to strongly connect the lives of these two men into the larger story of God's people in Luke-Acts. They are not simply a part of a similar plan, but are literally from the same ancestral lineage.

Birth and Growth of JBap (1:57–80)

Although the audience might expect the narrative to focus exclusively on Jesus at this point, Luke shifts the focus retrospectively back to JBap, describing his birth and growth. In this section, Zechariah delivers a prayer that reminds Luke's audience of many prophetic messages from the Hebrew Bible. Specifically, Zechariah states καὶ ἤγειρεν κέρας σωτηρίας ἡμῖν ἐν οἴκῳ Δαυὶδ παιδὸς αὐτοῦ, καθὼς ἐλάλησεν διὰ στόματος τῶν ἁγίων ἀπ᾽ αἰῶνος προφητῶν αὐτοῦ (1:69–70). This prayer connects JBap with the long line of prophetic witnesses speaking of God's salvation (1:71). JBap will himself be called προφήτης ὑψίστου (1:76).

The summary statement about JBap's growth (1:80) anticipates his public ministry as an adult, as well as anticipates Jesus' growth in 2:51–52. The fact that Luke describes JBap going to the wilderness until the day he appears publicly to Israel is seen by many as a literary creation to create a smoother transition from John's infancy narrative to his public ministry.[51] This verse also assists in interweaving the stories of JBap and Jesus as Luke first presents the account of Jesus' birth (2:1–52) prior to describing the public ministry of John in the wilderness (3:1–20).

Birth and Growth of Jesus (2:1–52)

As Luke's audience heard about the nature of Jesus' birth, they would again see the continuity between JBap and Jesus. But as before, the narrative of Jesus' birth creates more anticipation for what is to come than dwelling on what came before. The birth reports (1:57; 2:6) are patterned in part on Gen 25:24, and the accompanying reactions of joy and praise are closely

---

51. See Brown, *The Birth*, 376; Meier, *A Marginal Jew*, 2:27; Taylor, *The Immerser*, 42–45.

aligned. Likewise, the prophetic songs by Zechariah and Simeon/Anna share many linguistic parallels including: Holy Spirit (1:67; 2:26), Blessed is ... God (1:68; 2:28), redemption (1:68; 2:38), salvation (1:69, 71, 77; 2:30), and peace (1:79; 2:29). Both are circumcised and named appropriately (1:59–63; 2:21)[52] and each account is strategically brought up to the point where their public ministries will begin (1:80; 2:51–52).[53]

As Jesus is brought to the Temple, Simeon blesses Mary and Joseph with these words: "This child is destined for the falling and rising of many in Israel, and to be a sign that will be opposed so the inner thoughts of many will be revealed..." (2:34–35). With these words, Luke anticipates the rest of the narrative of God's salvation history, as he weaves together this legato story. There will be those who oppose God's plan even from within the house of Israel. Here, Luke anticipates how the character Jesus will be divisive in his upcoming ministry. Likewise, Luke explains how Israel can be divided because of Jesus and still serve as a continuation of God's work throughout Israel of the past.

Public Ministry of JBap Commences (Luke 3:1–20)

As the Lukan account moves past the Infancy Narratives toward the public ministries of JBap and Jesus, Joel Green notes how Luke "intricately integrates the accounts of birth and ministry preparation."[54] Specifically, he brings to mind JBap as "prophet of the Most High" (1:76) preparing the way for the Messiah, and Jesus as "Son of God" (1:35), an identity affirmed by God in 3:21-22. As Luke's audience encountered JBap's public ministry in Luke 3:2ff, they would have been immediately reminded of the infancy narratives. This reminder specifically occurs due to the word "wilderness" (1:80; 3:2), and because John is called "the son of Zechariah" (3:2) which draws attention back to God's intervention in the earlier birth narrative.[55] These connections demonstrate how Luke has utilized the birth narratives

---

52. Note how Luke goes to great lengths to parallel the naming of these two babies. Luke awkwardly inserts 2:21c to remind the hearer that Jesus, like JBap, was also given the name communicated by the angel before his birth. See Fearghail, *The Introduction*, 17.

53. Fearghail, *The Introduction*, 17.

54. Green, *The Gospel*, 159.

55. Ibid.

to adequately prepare his audience for the transition between JBap's public ministry and that of Jesus' in this narrative that follows.

As Luke narrates the public ministry of JBap, the audience is reminded of the many prophets presented throughout the Hebrew Bible. In the midst of JBap's message of repentance, the crowd becomes confused as to the identity of JBap, asking μήποτε αὐτὸς εἴη ὁ χριστός (3:15). Luke takes this opportunity for JBap himself to foreshadow the nature of Jesus' upcoming public ministry. JBap declares τὸ πτύον ἐν τῇ χειρὶ αὐτοῦ (3:17), again reconciling how a divided Israel can remain in continuity with Israel's past. After JBap's brief anticipatory comments of Jesus' public ministry, Luke's narrative describes the imprisonment of JBap as he gradually directs the focus toward Jesus.

Public Ministry of Jesus Commences (Luke 3:21—4:44)

Contra Conzelmann, the public ministries of JBap and Jesus are presented by Luke as complementary pieces of God's continuous salvific work. Some scholars have interpreted the imprisonment of JBap in Luke 3:20 as a distinct demarcation between the ministries of JBap and Jesus.[56] For example, Von Baer describes the separation between JBap and Jesus at 3:20–21 as a deliberate move on Luke's part to place Jesus alone at the center of the stage as the only bearer of the Spirit, and the leading figure in salvation history.[57] Likewise, Conzelmann finds in these verses Luke's intent to make clear the fundamental separation between JBap and Jesus despite their temporal overlap.[58] These analyses of the text, however, fail to take into account the larger transitional context of Luke 1:5—4:44. In fact, even while Herod has JBap placed in prison in 3:20, the narrative continues to describe his ministry of baptism in 3:21, and also Luke reintroduces JBap in Luke 7:18–35, offering more clarification concerning the complex relationship between these two individuals. In this way, Luke continues to weave the life of JBap with that of Jesus even while he is in prison. During JBap's public ministry, he connects Jesus with the Holy Spirit, and in 4:1 Jesus is described as "full of the Holy Spirit." Likewise, it is also telling that Luke has described Jesus as preparing for his public ministry by going straight to the wilderness,

---

56. It is notable that Luke does not describe the circumstances leading to JBap's imprisonment and death (Luke 3:19–20; cf. Mark 6:14–29; Matt 14:1–13).

57. Baer, *Heilige Geist*, 55–56.

58. Conzelmann, *The Theology*, 14–15.

where JBap had come from. It would appear that Jesus is preparing for public ministry in ways perhaps similar to those of JBap (1:80). It should also be noted that for Luke's audience, the fact that JBap has been locked up in prison would elicit questions surrounding what would then happen to the one greater than him, Jesus. The connections between these two create an inseparable bond.

Further, Fearghail notes parallels between Luke's presentation of JBap's public ministry and that of Jesus. Both individuals receive divine signals to begin their ministries (3:2; 3:21–22), and their paternity is mentioned at this point (3:2; 3:23). Both are presented as prophetic figures (3:2, 7–20; 4:16–30) who spend time in the desert prior to the inauguration of their ministries (3:2; 4:1–13). Both preach "good news" (3:18; 4:43) and their ministries demonstrate a fulfillment of Isaian prophecies (3:4-6; 4:18–19, 21).[59] Fearghail offers the following table of parallels:

3:2 Commission	3:21–22 Commission
3:2 Son of Zachariah	3:23–38 Son of Joseph; geneology
3:2 In the desert	4:1–13 In the desert; temptation
3:3-20 Ministry	4:14-44 Ministry
3:3 Scene of Ministry	4:14, 44 Scene of Ministry
3:4-6 Fulfills Isaian Prophecy	4:18-21 Fulfills Isaian Prophecy
3:7-19 Words (Deeds implied)	4:14-44 Words & Deeds
3:18 Preaching good news to people	4:43 Preaching good news of the Kingdom of God
3:20 "in prison"	4:44 In synagogues of Judea

As in the Infancy Narratives, Luke utilizes the parallels here not only to offer many similarities between JBap and Jesus, but also to bring their differences into sharper relief and navigate the audience forward toward the central character of Jesus. It becomes clear that JBap is simply a forerunner for Jesus, and his message of good news does not yet include the "Kingdom of God" as it does for Jesus (3:18; 4:43). Likewise, JBap's ministry begins with a familiar OT call ("word came to . . ."), while Jesus' ministry is inaugurated by an epiphany from heaven. It is also telling that the description of the public ministry of JBap (3:1–20) is significantly smaller than that of Jesus' public ministry (3:21—4:44) that follows.

Perhaps the most notable difference highlighted by Luke is that JBap's ministry is directed exclusively to Israel (1:16–17, 80), while Jesus' ministry

---

59. Fearghail, *The Introduction*, 29–30.

will transcend the borders of Israel because of its universal significance. Not only does Jesus explicitly describe a universal message (4:25–27), but Luke also elicits this through his shaping of Jesus' genealogy. Jesus' public ministry begins immediately with his genealogical record (3:23ff), and it is extremely telling that in this section, unlike Matthew's Gospel, Luke draws an ancestral line from Jesus back to the first man, Adam. Jesus is not just the continuation of Israelite heritage, but is the continuation of God's salvation history for all people universally. This has been previously hinted at by Luke through the universal setting of his birth narrative (2:1–2), the words of heavenly messengers (2:10, 14), and the words of Simeon (2:30–32). With the importance of genealogical records in antiquity, this certainly would make an impact upon Luke's Gentile audience, giving them assurance that they too are a continuation of God's work throughout history. Social memory theorists speak of this kind of strategy to connect individuals to a larger story from the past. Zerubavel states, "Rather than envision ourselves as disjointed atoms, knowing that we descend from some *common ancestor* makes us feel somehow 'connected.'"[60]

Conclusion

This chapter began with an examination of sources contemporary to Luke, which offered evidence that a variety of traditions surrounded JBap and Jesus. There was no one immutable version of these two individuals that had silenced the rest. Rather, these two important figures served as artifacts that were reusable for a variety of communities in the first century (and beyond). These two significant artifacts in early Christianity were commemorated for many reasons. Social memory theory describes how commemoration (through ritual or text or psychic identification) invites participation from the audience(s). Edward Casey states, "Commemorating does more than pay tribute to honorable actions undertaken in the past and at another place. It constructs the space, and continues the time, in which the commendably inter-human will be perduringly appreciated. Rather than looking back only, commemoration concerns itself with 'what lasting, comes toward us.'"[61] There was much at work during Luke's commemoration of these artifacts in nascent Christianity.

---

60. Zerubavel, *Time Maps*, 63.
61. Casey, *Remembering*, 247–48.

Through an examination of these varied traditions, it becomes clear that the early church struggled to understand the complex relationship between JBap and Jesus well into the second century. Many early Christian writings attempted to bridge the gap between JBap and Jesus, and while various solutions were offered, it is Luke who offers the most extensive treatment of the relationship between these two individuals. His elaborate rhetorical transition from JBap to Jesus spans four chapters, and intricately weaves the stories of these two men and their families together.

Why is Luke's particular commemoration of these events so uniquely arranged compared to contemporary accounts? It was discussed in chapter 2 that a primary reason for this rhetorical arrangement was due to the conventions of Greek historiography, an ancient genre that focused particular attention on bridging sections of the past together. However, it was also argued that Luke's particular rhetorical structure went beyond mere decorative convention. It has been argued in this chapter that the best explanation for Luke's unique commemoration was to present a connected narrative of Christianity's origins to affirm the identity of his late first-century audience(s). In this literary process, Luke has (re)shaped the traditions he received to form a more helpful arrangement for his largely Gentile audience. He has not only attempted to persuade his audience of the continuity from JBap to Jesus, but also to convince his listeners that the movement from traditional 2TP Judaism to the expanded mission of Jesus' ministry was not irreconcilable, but in fact a seamless transition. This is no small feat, which has resulted in this rather lengthy rhetorical bridge in Luke 1:5—4:44.

Luke has commemorated JBap and Jesus in a way that connected the traditions of his listening audience(s) to the larger continuous narrative of salvation history. Their story has been modified and enlarged, resulting in a more connected understanding of past events. Social memory theory, therefore, augments more traditional historical methods to provide a more detailed portrait of what Luke was trying to accomplish in his two-volume project.

4

The Transition from Jesus to His Disciples

As Luke's audience remembered the transition from Jesus to his followers, many mental gaps remained for them. As they examined their staccato traditions, questions arose as to why Jesus bypassed the current Jewish leadership structure available to him in favor of appointing common followers to places of prominence. The Twelve Apostles were not rhetorically trained, nor of a priestly class,[1] yet Jesus selected them to lead God's people and then subsequently expanded his mission to an even wider pool of disciples (including the Seventy-two and even women). The failures of Jesus' disciples in previous traditions (namely Mark's Gospel)[2] would have caused confusion regarding this transition of authority. Luke, therefore, will spend a considerable amount of effort constructing an elaborate rhetorical transition, demonstrating the fluid continuity between Jesus and his followers. In the process, Luke will attempt to persuade his audience(s) that this was a divinely sanctioned transition.

This chapter will begin with a brief look at how Luke's audience(s) would have likely remembered Jesus' closest group of disciples, The Twelve Apostles. How would the late first-century church have understood the relationship between Jesus and his immediate followers? Once this is addressed, I will turn my attention to the Lukan Gospel. I will demonstrate that Luke has crafted an elaborate rhetorical transition to persuade his audience that God orchestrated a fluid continuity between Jesus and his many

---

1. See Acts 4:13.
2. In Mark's Gospel more than the other canonical gospels, the failures of the disciples come to the forefront (4:13, 40; 6:50–52; 7:18; 8:14–21; 10:13–14, 35–45), even though Jesus offers them much private instruction (4:10–13, 33–34; 7:17–18; 9:28–29; 10:11–12; 13:3–37). Eventually, all Jesus' disciples desert him (14:50; 14:72; 16:8).

disciples. In this way, the Lukan Jesus paves the way for a new leadership structure that removes traditional boundaries.

Jesus' Disciples Remembered in Tradition

Since the Twelve Apostles are representative of the wider circle of Jesus' followers in early Christian literature, it will be helpful to examine how they were portrayed in the time period surrounding Luke's Gospel. This will provide a good indication of how Luke's audience(s) would have likely remembered the transition between Jesus and his followers. While some scholars attempt to deny the historical existence of the Twelve Apostles,[3] this chapter will affirm the conclusions of the majority of scholarship that an inner group among Jesus' disciples actually existed.[4] This is a significant assumption, because it will be demonstrated that Luke's audiences struggled to properly place the Twelve Apostles within a coherent narrative of actual historical events.

Therefore, operating under the assumption that a set group of Twelve Apostles existed during the earthly ministry of Jesus, it will be important to now note how these individuals were remembered at the end of the first century. What historically happens to the Twelve after Jesus' ministry remains somewhat of a mystery. While the book of Acts describes some information regarding the more significant disciples, it is limited and there is no data offered following the Council at Jerusalem (Acts 15). Tradition has certainly attempted to fill in the gaps about the later lives of the Twelve Apostles, but these accounts are of limited historical value.[5] While the historical details are vague in these later accounts, it can be observed that the second-century church still struggled with the place of Jesus' disciples in larger salvation history. For example, *Acts of Peter* (ca. 150–200 CE) describes Peter refusing to flee from Agrippa, when everyone else is escaping to protect their lives.[6] It would appear that the author of this document is attempting to counter the apparent cowardice of the Twelve at the crucifixion of Jesus as described in Mark 14:50 (ἔφυγον πάντες).

---

3. Funk, *The Acts of Jesus*, 71.

4. Meier, *Companions*, 98–106. See also his earlier article, "The Circle," 635–72. McKnight, "Jesus and the Twelve," 185–89. Sanders, *Jesus and Judaism*, 101.

5. See, for example, *Ascen. Isa.* 4.2–3; *Apoc. Pet.* 14:4; *Acts Pet.* 35–40; Lactantius, *Mort.* 2:5–8; Jerome, *Vir. ill.* 1.

6. *Acts Pet.* 35.

The Transition from Jesus to His Disciples

It will be helpful here to briefly examine the presentation of the disciples in the other canonical gospels to observe how the late first-century church understood the position of Jesus' disciples in the early church. The Gospel of Mark offers the most distinct presentation of the disciples in the NT. After a somewhat positive description of these men initially, the rest of the Gospel describes the sustained failures of the Twelve, highlighting their spiral downward as the Markan narrative progresses.[7] By the end of the Gospel, all of Jesus' disciples have deserted him at his crucifixion (14:50–52) and they are left in silence and fear at Mark's abrupt conclusion. It is hardly surprising that in the century following Mark's Gospel, scribes felt compelled to append a "proper" ending in order to smooth over this seeming discontinuity between Jesus and his followers.

Matthew's Gospel shows numerous signs that Mark's treatment of discipleship was insufficient. With a focus on Jesus as *revealer*, this Gospel spends much more time in didactic content,[8] suggesting that Mark has not offered enough teaching content to shape discipleship. Likewise, Matthew removes some of the negative characterization of the Twelve, portraying a generally more positive portrait of these men. For example, Matthew softens the ambition of James and John by having their mother pose the question to Jesus (Matt 10:20; Mark 10:35). Likewise, Matthew deletes the disciples' question after the Transfiguration concerning what it meant to rise from the dead (Matt 17:9; Mark 9:10). Similarly, Matthew's disciples behave more appropriately during the various boat scenes. While Mark's disciples wake Jesus with the accusatory question, "Teacher, do you not care that we are perishing? (Mark 4:38), Matthew's disciples respectfully pray, "Lord, save us! We are perishing!" (Matt 8:25). This is just to name a few of the various Matthean redactions of Mark's Gospel. However, it is important to note that Matthew is still bound by tradition with regard to the various failures of the disciples.[9] While the general portrait of the disciples in Matthew's Gospel is much more positive than in his Markan source, one still finds a mix of affirmative and critical remarks surrounding the Twelve.[10] In the midst of this mixed portrait, Matthew does spend more time than Mark demonstrating

---

7. Carter, "The Disciples," 88.

8. Specifically, Matthew includes five primary blocks of teaching materials (5–7, 10, 13, 18, 24–25).

9. See Matt 8:23–27; 10:7–8; 14:13–21 15:16–17, 32–39; 16:5–12; 17:16, 19; 19:13; 20:20–24; 26:36–46, 56.

10. Carter, "The Disciples," 97.

how the disciples will play a significant role in the post-resurrection era (17:9; 18:18–20; 19:28; 24:14; 27:64; 28:16–20).[11]

The Gospel of John only mentions the "Twelve" four times (6:67, 70, 71; 20:24), but frequently utilizes the term "disciples" to refer to a group of Jesus' followers that extends beyond the Twelve.[12] One particular individual, whom the Fourth Gospel designates as the "Beloved Disciple" serves as the model disciple, following Jesus in a close and believing relationship (13:23; 19:26-27; 21;7,20).[13] Despite the somewhat idealized portrait of Jesus' ministry developed in the Fourth Gospel, the author still includes the occasional shortcomings of Jesus' disciples, as they struggle to understand his identity and mission. A major focus of discipleship in the Fourth Gospel is the testimony of Jesus' identity. During the unique Farewell Discourse (John 14–17), Jesus highlights how his followers are to be his witnesses by continuing his work and teaching. During this Farewell message, Jesus describes the Holy Spirit as the primary instrument to assist the disciples in their future work, as they are incapable of carrying on Jesus' ministry without divine assistance.

While the three canonical Gospels described above contain some differences in historical details, they all demonstrate that the disciples were remembered as imperfect and heavily reliant on Jesus for understanding and insight. Mark's Gospel presents the most critical portrait of the disciples, which is seen to be embarrassing in later accounts (Matthew, John, and Luke). However, while later accounts certainly smooth over some of the embarrassing failures by the Twelve, they all seem to be bound by a tradition that recognized the shortcomings of this group.

Lukan Remembrances of Jesus and His Disciples

This chapter has thus far examined how Jesus' disciples were remembered at the end of the first century. This has helped to establish the rhetorical exigency that motivated Luke to shape his narrative arrangement as it stands. Previous traditions had not adequately explained the transition of leadership from Jesus to his disciples, creating a need for the Lukan transition spanning the middle third of his Gospel. The rest of this chapter will

11. Longenecker, "Taking Up the Cross Daily," 55.

12. Carter, "The Disciples," 100. This is evident from John 6:66: "From this time on, many of his disciples turned back and no longer followed him."

13. Longenecker, "Taking Up the Cross Daily," 56.

focus on this elaborate Lukan transition that bridges the ministry of Jesus to that of his disciples. In this transition, Luke persuades his audience of the continuity between Jesus' ministry and that of his many followers (including the Twelve and the Seventy-two and the wider group of followers as described in Acts).

It has been widely recognized in Lukan scholarship that some type of literary transition occurs around Luke 9:51 that bridges Jesus' Galilean ministry (4:14—9:50) with his journey toward Jerusalem (9:51—19:27). John Nolland sees Luke 9:21–50 as "transitional," preparing the reader for the Travel Narrative which begins in 9:51.[14] Charles H. Talbert views Luke 9:18–50 as a prelude to the journey toward Jerusalem, functioning as a basis for the Travel Narrative.[15] Joel B. Green observes, "The closing of the Galilean section of the Third Gospel and the commencement of the journey narrative is marked definitively in 9:51–56 with the fourfold use of the word 'to journey' and the repeated references to Jesus' determination to go to Jerusalem."[16] David P. Moessner sees Luke 9:1–50 as a preview of the journey of the Mosaic prophet, which occurs in 9:51—19:44.[17]

While these types of structural analyses above differ on some minor issues, there is a general consensus in which some portion of Luke 9 leads up to a clear transitional break at 9:51. What is lacking in Lukan structural analyses, however, is a detailed treatment of the larger surrounding rhetorical transition that explains the transfer of authority from Jesus to his disciples. In this chapter, I will suggest a widening of this primary transition in the Lukan Gospel to stretch from Jesus' Galilean ministry to the Lukan travel narrative. It will be demonstrated that this large transitional segment serves to offer Luke's audience reassurance of the newly developed leadership structure. Jesus has chosen the most unlikely of followers to carry on his ministry, and Luke's audience needed to understand that this remained firmly a part of God's divine plan.

Jesus will make his way from Galilee to Jerusalem, but not for the reason that many would expect. He does not journey to Jerusalem to support

---

14. Nolland, *Luke*, 1:448. He sees 9:18–20 as a culmination of Jesus' entire Galilean ministry beginning at 4:14.

15. Talbert, *Reading Luke*, 117–19. He sees a chiastic structure from 9:51—19:44, in which its central focus is the killing of prophets in 13:31–35.

16. Green, *The Gospel*, 399. He also highlights the failures of the disciples in Luke 9:37–50 which produce the narrative need for the long journey in 9:51—19:48, whose central focus is the "formation of perceptive, faithful disciples" (ibid, 387).

17. Moessner, *Lord of the Banquet*.

the current elitist leadership structure of chief priests and religious leaders.[18] Rather he spends this journey training a rather unorthodox group of disciples (by normal Jewish standards) in a leadership style quite contradictory to that of the current Jewish system. This rhetorical transition, therefore, serves as the introduction of a new leadership structure, one composed not only of the Twelve, but one that would extend far beyond an elitist group to the Seventy-two (and all the geographical and ethnic expansion that this stood for). This new leadership structure would even go so far as to offer a place to women as Jesus' disciples, a practice largely unheard of in traditional Jewish circles. The type of leadership structure that is developed by Jesus is one of *imitatio Christi* in which his identity as a suffering servant is to be embraced by anyone desiring to become a leader in the restored Israel. This would have addressed a significant discontinuity in the minds of Luke's audience, who were still struggling to understand the staccato-like shift in leadership from the Jewish elite to Jesus' disciples. It is no surprise that it would take some time for his audience to follow his argument, and thus he establishes an elaborate rhetorical transition to facilitate this persuasion. The rhetorical structure of this legato transition is as follows:

A	Jesus' Galilean Ministry	5:1—8:56
b	Jesus Calls Disciples	6:12–49
a	Jesus' Galilean Ministry Resumed	7:1—8:56
B	Jesus Commissions Disciples to Replace Traditional Jewish Leadership Structure	9:1—18:17

As has been discussed in previous chapters, a rhetorical transition can take a variety of forms, so long as there is an *overlap of material* between the two main text units. This overlap is precisely what one sees in the A-b-a/B structure above. As this structure highlights, this is a crucial juncture in Luke's narrative in which Jesus gradually transfers his ministry to his disciples. While the disciples are introduced during Jesus' Galilean ministry (Luke 6:13–16), they do not take an active role until Luke 9:1. Since the primary shift from Jesus to his disciples occurs in Luke 9–10, it would stand to reason that this section would provide explicit information regarding the type of leadership structure that Jesus desires from his disciples. This is precisely what is found, as Luke 9:11–51 describes how Jesus' identity as

---

18. In fact, Jesus' primary conflict with the religious authorities is over the issue of "authority" and who will rule God's people. See Kingsbury, *Conflict in Luke*, 109.

one who must suffer and die is the template for the new leaders of a restored Israel. In this way, Luke intimately connects the disciples' mission to that of their predecessor Jesus, developing his version of a legato salvation history, free from "humps or hollows."

In what follows, I will examine each of the sections of the rhetorical transition itemized above. Within each section, I will describe how Luke has stylized this rhetorical juncture to steer his audience toward a proper understanding of the continuity between Jesus and the leadership structure he developed through his disciples.

Jesus' Galilean Ministry (Luke 5:1–8:56)

Jesus' Galilean ministry has begun to divide ethnic Israel into those who accept his prophetic message and those who do not. Johnson notes that while the marginalized have accepted him and become his disciples, this prophet is being rejected by the religious elite, the current leadership of Israel. Johnson rightly notes that this has created "a leadership vacuum," posing the question, "Who will be the leaders of this people?"[19] This is precisely the question that Luke intends to answer in this elaborate rhetorical transition. Luke will demonstrate that it is Jesus who seamlessly transfers his power and authority to the Twelve (and beyond; cf. 72 in Luke 10), preparing a new leadership structure for the restored Israel.

Jesus Calls Disciples (Luke 6:12–49)

While Jesus has called a few individuals to be disciples, they have served no real role in the narrative until this point. This passage serves a key rhetorical function for Luke in introducing the Twelve.[20] It is here where Luke first designates these twelve men as "apostles," a term that held great significance for Luke compared to the other canonical Gospel writers. While each of the other gospel writers only include the term "apostles" once (Mark 6:30; Matt 10:2; and John 13:16), the term appears six times in the Gospel of Luke (6:13; 9:10; 11:49; 17:5; 22:14; 24:10) and thirty times in the Acts of the Apostles. Longenecker states, "For Luke, the church is only faithful

---

19. Johnson, *The Gospel*, 147.

20. Green rightly notes that Luke 6:12–16 serves a "transitional" function. Green, *The Gospel*, 257.

to its calling as it perseveres in the teaching and tradition of the apostles, who constitute the human link with Jesus. And Christian discipleship is only authentic as it does likewise."[21] It is significant that the term "apostles" first appears at Luke 6:13, marking a transition into the role of these twelve throughout the rest of the Gospel. The next place this term appears is in Luke 9:10, precisely where the narrative shifts focus to the leadership development of Jesus' disciples.

It is here in this passage that Luke prepares his audience for the future leadership of these individuals and demonstrates that their selection was divinely sanctioned. Joel Green states, "As Luke presents it, the *idea* of choosing itself, the election of *twelve* persons, and the choice of *these particular persons* from among the larger group of disciples—all three are divinely sanctioned. Jesus thus acts as God's agent and in continuity with the divine will."[22] It is also notable that Jesus receives this direction on a mountain in a similar manner in which God will speak to Jesus again on the mountain in 9:28–37, at the precise point when God asks the Apostles to listen to his son Jesus in order to adequately lead a restored Israel. As Jesus comes down the mountain in both passages, the Greek shows parallels (6:17: Καὶ καταβὰς μετ' αὐτῶν ἔστη ἐπὶ τόπου πεδινοῦ, καὶ ὄχλος πολὺς μαθητῶν αὐτοῦ and 9:37: κατελθόντων αὐτῶν ἀπὸ τοῦ ὄρους συνήντησεν αὐτῷ ὄχλος πολύς).

Based on the specific narrative context of this passage, namely the theme of opposition in 5:1—6:11, Luke seems determined to introduce these twelve men as a replacement for Israel's current leadership. Green states, "With scribes and Pharisees responding to Jesus with misapprehension and anger, the choosing of the twelve signals a judgment on Israel's leadership for their lack of insight into God's redemptive plan and compassionate care for those in need."[23] Also, the symbolic importance of the Twelve for Luke cannot be overestimated, as Luke emphasizes the specific number of apostles in order to highlight how these men will lead a renewed Israel.[24] Green also notes the relatively minor role of most of the Twelve in

---

21. Longenecker, "Taking Up the Cross Daily," 59.

22. Green, *The Gospel*, 258.

23. Ibid., 259.

24. See the emphasis placed on replacing Judas in Acts 1:1-2, 15-26 to maintain *twelve* apostles.

the larger narrative of Luke-Acts as evidence for the symbolic importance of the number twelve.[25]

Likewise, considering the surrounding context, it is important to note that many found discontinuities between Jesus' disciples and the disciples of the Pharisees (5:33). Luke 5:33–35 suggests that a more logical transition would have been from Jesus to the Pharisees, instead of developing the leadership of the Twelve Apostles.[26] While fasting seems to be the primary discontinuity mentioned in this passage, there were certainly many reasons why it would be more logical to transfer authority from Jesus to the current Jewish leadership. However, Jesus is clear that new wine requires new wineskins (5:37), highlighting a reconstruction of leadership structure for the church to come.[27]

Once the Lukan Jesus has demonstrated through prayer that the Twelve Apostles (and not the current Jewish leadership) establish a continuity with Jesus' ministry (6:12–16), Jesus moves on to present a succinct lesson on discipleship that will further justify God's decision to place these men in leadership positions. It is important to note that these teachings were directed toward his disciples (6:20). This didactic material in 6:17–49 offers Luke's audience a brief introduction to a new leadership structure, anticipating the longer discipleship teachings that will resume in Luke 9:1—18:17. However, before Luke moves to his extended Central Section, he pauses to give his audience some time to process this new leadership of the Twelve.

Jesus' Galilean Ministry Resumed (Luke 7:1—8:56)

Following the anticipatory passage of Luke 6:12–49, Jesus resumes his Galilean ministry right where he left off in Luke 5. Only now Jesus' disciples have entered into his ministry, despite playing a relatively minor role until Luke 9:1. While his disciples remain rather passive here, Luke lets his audiences know that this section includes both the Twelve as well as the introduction of women into Jesus' ministry.

This section serves to give the audience time to synthesize Jesus with the newly introduced group of Twelve Apostles (6:12–16) prior to their

---

25. Green, *The Gospel*, 259; Jervell, *Luke*, 86–87.

26. Marshall, *The Gospel*, 223.

27. Luke is also utilizing this section to prepare his hearers for the transition from fasting to feasting that will occur in the Travel Narrative.

commissioning. The disciples observe Jesus as bystanders at this point in the narrative, while Jesus continues his ministry as he did prior to the calling of the Twelve. Despite some "anticipatory" elements in this section of text,[28] the primary "center of gravity" lies in Jesus' Galilean ministry.

This section also gives the audience time to synthesize the idea that Jesus' successors not only includes the Twelve, but also an expanded group of disciples that includes women as well. At multiple instances in this section, Jesus breaks traditional Jewish purity boundaries to minister to women.[29] In addition, women are introduced in Luke 8:1–3 who accompany Jesus during his Galilean ministry and provide financially for his ministry.[30] While Jesus continues his Galilean ministry at this point, this ministry has incorporated an expanded following that stands in contrast to traditional Jewish standards.

Jesus Commissions Disciples to Replace Traditional Jewish Leadership Structure (Luke 9:1—18:17)

The Commissioning of the Twelve marks a significant turning point in this Lukan narrative. This section inaugurates the journey ahead, and it is at this point that Jesus begins to firmly impose his identity upon his followers. It is not until Luke 9:1ff that Jesus' disciples become thoroughly entrenched in Jesus' mission, making this section of text a key rhetorical juncture to Luke's early hearers. Prior to this juncture in the narrative, Jesus' disciples are left primarily as background characters. Disciples appear in 5:30, 33; 6:1, but as Joel Green describes them, they are merely "stage props" early in the narrative.[31] While Jesus specifically selects twelve particular disciples from among his many followers (Luke 6:13–16), Jesus offers them no responsibilities until 9:1ff. It would appear that in Luke's reworking of his primary source, Mark, he has postponed the responsibilities of the Twelve until later in the story. Mark 3:14–15 records that Jesus "appointed twelve . . . to be with him, and to be sent out to proclaim the message and to have

---

28. Such as Jesus clarifying what true "kinship" looks like (8:19–21) and teaching his disciples to increase their faith while at sea (8:22–25).

29. For example, see the healing of the widow's son at Nain (7:11–17), the woman with the alabaster jar of perfume (7:36–50), Jairus' daughter (8:41–42; 49–56), and the bleeding woman (8:43–48).

30. Witherington, *Women*, 116–18.

31. Green, *The Theology*, 103.

authority to exorcise demons." To the contrary, Luke 6:13 simply records that Jesus "chose twelve of them whom he also named apostles." The mission is postponed until Luke 9 in order to include an anticipatory element of the chain link transition and to give the audience time to process the continuity between Jesus and his immediate disciples.

In the beginning stages of the Lukan story, it is Jesus' healing ministry in Galilee that is primarily emphasized. Even by chapter 8, Luke must remind the listeners that the Twelve are still with Jesus during his itinerant campaign throughout Galilee. It is not until here in chapter 9 that Jesus begins to share some of the spotlight with his disciples, as he commissions the Twelve for a specific task. Jesus offers the Twelve the same authority that he himself had just demonstrated in the previous scenes, namely curing diseases and healing the demon-possessed (cf. 8:1–56). It appears as if Luke encourages the audience to know that the disciples are now being integrated into the mission as Jesus' successors. Johnson notes that while Luke follows his Markan source (Mark 6:6–16 and 6:32–44; omitting the story of John's beheading in Mark 6:17–29), his careful editing of the three scenes in Luke 9:1–17 shows his audience how consciously he has shaped this narrative section around the future role of the Twelve as the prophetic successors of Jesus.[32]

In chapters 9 and 10, Luke describes a set of characteristics that will exemplify this new leadership style of the Twelve. These traits are then elaborated upon in Luke's Central Section that follows (Luke 11–18). It should come as no surprise that it is Jesus who is demonstrating these various attributes for his followers, developing continuity between his ministry and theirs, and at the same time contrasting this new leadership style with the existing worldly leadership paradigm. Since this was such a monumental shift in the leadership structure of God's people, Luke spends an excessive amount of space drawing comparisons between the existing worldly paradigm and Jesus' new model for his disciples. Therefore, the remainder of this chapter will focus on these comparisons.

The first distinctive feature of this new leadership style is an outward focus, as Luke shifts the focus from an inward, centrifugal mission to an outward, centripetal mission.[33] It is important to understand that 2TP Judaism was generally not involved in formally sending missionar-

---

32. Johnson, *The Gospel*, 148.

33. Aaron Kuecker describes this shift as a move to an "allocentric identity" (Kuecker, *The Spirit*, 18).

ies in order to disseminate their message.[34] Scholarship in the past fifty years has rightly challenged the traditional opinion that 2TP Judaism was involved in active proselytization.[35] Notable among these to overturn the previous majority opinion are Martin Goodman, Scot McKnight, Edmund Will, and Claude Orrieux.[36] Since these seminal works, scholarship has dramatically shifted to the view that little to no Jewish mission occurred in 2TP Judaism.[37] For the most part, 2TP Judaism was attempting to firm up their own identity in order to avoid complete assimilation into Roman Hellenism. While there did exist a belief in a universal ingathering, this was only to occur at the eschaton and not at the present time (Isa 66:18–19). This inward focus of 2TP Judaism contrasts with the actions initiated by Jesus in Luke 9:1ff. He is not waiting for some period in the future for the diffusion of God's Kingdom. Jesus is radically reshaping the social structure of the Jewish community in his commissioning of the Twelve throughout Galilee.[38] Contrary to the previous Jewish leadership regime, the newly appointed leadership structure will develop an outward mission that will become core to their purpose. Since this would remain an extremely challenging paradigm shift, Luke has rhetorically shaped his narrative to include two outward missions: the Twelve in 9:1–10 and the Seventy-Two in 10:1–16. This allows his listening audience time to reconcile these dramatic shifts in the early Christian movement.

Luke also clarifies this new outwardly-focused leadership style through his reversal of the traditional Jewish pilgrimage in the Commission accounts (Luke 9–10). Bovon points out that throughout this mission, Jesus is "radically transvaluing the goal, the content, and the conditions of traditional pilgrimage."[39] He goes on to state, "Instead of going up to Jeru-

---

34. There does seem to be some pockets of diaspora Judaism that did actively attempt the diffusion of their message into their culture, but there existed no centralized effort at active proselytization. See, for example: Philo, *De Virtutibus* 102–3, in *On the Special Laws, Book 4*; *Special Laws* 1.320–23 in *On the Decalogue. On the Special Laws, Books 1–3*; Horace, *Sat.* 1.4.138–43; Juvenal, *Sat.* 6.542–44.

35. For a nice summary concerning this debate, see Keener, *Acts*, 505–17.

36. Goodman, *Mission and Conversion*; McKnight, *A Light*; Will and Orrieux, *Proselytisme juif?*.

37. Schnabel, *Early Christian Mission*, 1:173.

38. It is clear that the Third Gospel writer grounds the Gentile mission in the earthly ministry of Jesus. For work in this field, see the following: Bird, *Jesus*; Wilson, *The Gentiles*; Schnabel, *Early Christian Mission*, 21.

39. Bovon, *Luke*, 345.

salem, one goes to the dispersed children of Israel; instead of fulfilling one's own religious duty, one brings the new message to others. Instead of a pilgrim's equipment, one wears the minimalist outfit of the last days.... [M]issionary travel would achieve a liturgical significance. The missionary would sanctify the profane sphere of the house by his or her activity. The quality of the holy would reach humanity in worldliness, and people would no longer enter the holy Temple."[40] This transfer of holiness from a specific location (the Temple) to a mobile human being presents unlimited potential to all sorts of social groups that did not previously exist. This would, therefore, usher in a more universal Kingdom than was previously perceived by the religious elites. Jesus is reversing much about the traditional Jewish leadership structure of his day.

In an agonistic culture such as first-century Roman Hellenism, communities and religious groups would find themselves resistant to outsiders.[41] Those involved in this type of society would naturally find themselves resistant to a universal mission embracing a variety of social levels. The disciples are not immune to such self-absorption, as they found themselves concerned with their own self-importance and keeping healing powers within their particular in-group (9:46–50). To allow others to heal would jeopardize the infrastructure of their operation.[42] To combat this centripetal attitude, the Lukan Jesus sends out his disciples into the foreign land of Samaria to befriend these outsiders (9:52–55). In this way, there is an attempt in the narrative to remove strict ethnic boundaries on the way toward a universal mission.[43] Jesus also makes it very clear that this universal Kingdom of God will take precedence over any other group boundaries that may exist.[44] These radical requirements advocated by Jesus in Luke 9:57–62 even places one's Kingdom identity in a more salient position than one's family and kinship identity.[45]

---

40. Ibid.

41. Malina, *The New Testament World*, 36.

42. This worldly attitude is reminiscent of those in Jesus' hometown of Nazareth (Luke 4:23–30) who seem solely concerned to keep the miraculous powers of Jesus within their own small community.

43. Ethnic division was highly significant in antiquity, as evidenced in the work of Herodotus. Herodotus, *The Persian Wars*, 8.144. These salient ethnic boundaries were also highlighted in ancient cartography.

44. Nolland, *Luke*, 544–45.

45. No part of the first-century Mediterranean world was untouched by the family institution. In this ancient society, kinship could hardly be separated from religion and

In order to further establish the movement toward a universal mission, Luke narrates the Commissioning of the Seventy(-two) in Luke 10:1–16. While there are many similarities between the two commissioning accounts, there are also differences that highlight a greatly expanded mission. It has been widely recognized in Lukan scholarship that this expansion from the Twelve to the seventy-two reorients Luke's audience toward a universal mission.[46] The Twelve no longer have exclusive rights to this universal mission, but instead this is to be a mission involving all of Jesus' disciples. Whether the original Lukan work contained "seventy" disciples or "seventy-two," this is a clear allusion to the Table of Nations in Gen. 10, where the MT contains seventy names, and the LXX has seventy-two. This allusion to the Table of Nations (with its outward focus) again points toward the expanded boundaries of God's people. No longer are Israelite insiders to receive privileged treatment among the nations of the world. The scope of this mission has been enlarged to include outsiders. In this way, this commission foreshadows the universal mission in Luke's second volume.[47] This is further emphasized after sending the seventy(-two) by the macarism: Blessed are the eyes that see what you see! For I tell you that many prophets and kings desired to see what you see but did not see it, and to hear what you hear, but did not hear it" (10:23–24). Not only is Jesus inaugurating a universal mission, but is enlisting a growing number of followers in leadership positions. Jesus is clearly reconstructing a new leadership paradigm for a restored Israel.[48]

In addition to an outward focus, Luke also characterizes this new leadership structure through a redefinition of purity boundaries. This narrative steers Luke's contemporary audience toward a mission focused on the socially marginalized (and hence, under the power of "evil" and in need of a "cure").[49] It is these socially marginalized in society who receive significant attention in the Lukan narrative. No longer to be excluded from God's mission, the Lukan narrative initiates them back into the community of God's people. In the Jewish worldview, anyone with some physical defect or disease would have been excluded from the Temple. In their development

---

politics, as it was the primary institution of concern. Hanson and Oakman, *Palestine*, 21. See also Malina, *New Testament World*, 29

46. Nolland, *Luke*, 549. Bovon, *Luke*, 343.
47. Talbert, *Reading Luke*, 122.
48. Johnson, *The Gospel*, 161.
49. Compare to Jesus' focus in his initial speech in Luke 4:18–19.

of *halakah*, Jewish leadership developed rigorous hedges around the Law, which prevented many from entering the Temple. For example, while Lev. 21:16–21 describes requirements that priests remain physically unblemished when entering the Temple, first-century Jewish leadership applied these restrictions to the entire Jewish community. It is important to realize that to be denied access to the Temple not only severed one from religious situations, but also removed one from a major center of community life. Through this healing described in Luke 9:1–2, the Twelve are restoring the marginalized and alienated back into the people of God.[50] In this way, Jesus inaugurates a new priestly leadership.

For Luke, redefining purity boundaries for his newly appointed leadership was highlighted most clearly through his description of meals. Every culture has particular social boundaries that mark off acceptable procedures in everyday life, and food is one aspect of this.[51] Green describes the significance of food boundaries in the first century: "In the ancient Mediterranean world, mealtime was a social event whose significance far outdistanced the need to satisfy one's hunger. To welcome people at the table had become tantamount to extending to them intimacy, solidarity, acceptance; table companions were treated as though they were of one's extended family. Sharing food encoded messages about hierarchy, inclusion and exclusion, boundaries and crossing boundaries. Who ate with whom, where one sat in relation to whom at the table—such questions as these were charged with social meaning in the time of Jesus and Luke."[52] In an era where mealtimes were so strongly charged with social implications, one can understand the desire of the disciples to send away the crowds of thousands to establish some order in Luke 9. On the contrary, the only organization Jesus seems concerned about was getting these large crowds into groups of fifty for easier food distribution (9:14). This is clearly a recategorization of normal ethnic, economic, and religious boundaries. Bruce Malina speaks of certain "social maps" of the Jewish community in the first century, including space, time, people, and things, and meals.[53] In Luke's Feeding of the Five Thousand, Jesus has restructured all five of these social

---

50. Green, *Theology*, 96.
51. Douglas, "Deciphering a Meal," 249–75.
52. Green, *Theology*, 87.
53. Malina and Rohrbaugh, *Social-Science Commentary*, 396.

maps. Proper purity rules have taken a subsidiary position under Jesus and his message of the Kingdom (9:11).[54]

This miraculous feeding anticipates the prominent place of the ancient meal motif in Luke's Central Section, as Luke will continue to highlight the expanded participation in this new Kingdom community. If the primary purpose of the Travel Narrative is to explain a new leadership structure in God's Kingdom, Luke's literary use of the communal meal should come as no surprise. The communal meal was one of the primary means of social stratification in the ancient world and Luke desired to highlight Jesus' re-structuring of this entire institution.[55]

Many scholars have connected the Feeding of the 5000 (9:11–17) with the Last Supper (Luke 22) in the Lukan narrative.[56] For example, a Lukan omission of a Markan reference to the two fish would seem to be an effort to maintain ties between this account and the Eucharist (Mark 6:41; Luke 9:16). Since, for this gospel writer, his Eucharist presentation ushers in a universal banquet of the Kingdom, it would be a logical conclusion to assume he is attempting to make similar connections in the "Feeding of the 5000."[57] In other words, the narrative uses the "Feeding of the 5000" as a foreshadowing of a universal church at the eschatological banquet table with Jesus.[58]

Another way Luke characterized this new leadership style was his focus on God as one's sole provision. Unlike the wealthy Jewish aristocracy, Luke records Jesus' directive to "take nothing for your journey" (9:3).[59] There have been several reasons suggested for this first directive given to the Twelve at their commissioning,[60] but the most solid reason for this instruction seems to be a concentrated focus on God's provision.[61] The Twelve would need to

---

54. In this way, Luke foreshadows the restructuring of purity regulations introduced in Acts 10.

55. For information on the ancient communal meal see the following: Dunbabin, *The Roman Banquet*; Smith, *From Symposium to Eucharist*; Smith, "Table Fellowship," 613–38; Smith and Taussig, *Meals*; Taussig, *In the Beginning*.

56. Talbert, "The Lukan Presentation," 492–97. O'Toole also provides a helpful chart of parallels between Luke 9 and 22–23. O'Toole, "Luke's Message," 89.

57. Hahn, "Kingdom and Church," 308.

58. Bovon, *Luke*, 353.

59. In this Lukan account, Jesus instructs them to take nothing for their mission, a stricter command than that given by Jesus in the Markan parallel (Mark 6:8).

60. Bovon, *Luke*, 345; Nolland, *Luke*, 429.

61. This seems clear from Jesus' elaboration in Luke 22:35. See Bovon, *Luke*, 343–45.

The Transition from Jesus to His Disciples

rely on God for basic food needs and also lodging on their itinerant mission throughout Galilee. Hospitality protocol in the ancient world made it extremely challenging to find lodging with strangers, which would have placed Jesus' disciples in a highly vulnerable position.[62] Jesus is cultivating leaders who will understand a deep reliance on God for essentials, which would draw a sharp contrast with the wealthy Jewish aristocracy.

Another manner in which Luke shifts the leadership style away from the current Jewish regime (as well as the general Greco-Roman leadership model) was through a focus on servanthood and humility. Luke focuses his narrative on the passion predictions of Jesus and the humiliation that accompanies such an identity. In order to accomplish this emphasis, Luke departs from his Markan source by omitting 6:45—8:26.[63] This section in Mark develops the incomprehension of the disciples, and Luke has quite a different strategy in mind with his narrative arrangement. Johnson notes, "He [Luke] connects the sequence here directly to the sending of the Twelve and the multiplication of the loaves, thereby compressing the narrative and fixing its focus on the Twelve as the new leaders of the restored Israel."[64] Luke goes to great lengths to omit the incomprehension of the disciples, most notably the exclusion of the objection and rebuke of Peter (Luke 9:20–21; cf. Mark 8:29–33). It is precisely at this point of the transfer of power that Jesus explains that leadership will no longer be characterized by hierarchy and position, but rather by servanthood and suffering. Jesus goes on to answer the question of Jesus' identity posed by Herod back in Luke 9:7–9. However, the emphasis of the narrative is more than a simple historical statement of Jesus' identification. He wishes to remove any notions of worldly power and instead develop a spirit of humble service in his followers. While Jesus is passing on leadership to his followers, there will be no room for pride or hierarchical boundaries.

This replacement of worldly concepts of power with humility is most vividly seen in the juxtaposition of the Transfiguration account with the second passion prediction. The scholar who has produced the most significant work on the Lukan Transfiguration narrative is David P. Moessner.[65] Moessner correctly observes the centrality of the Transfiguration (9:28–36) in presenting Jesus' identity and providing the authority for Jesus' prophetic

---

62. Grimshaw, *The Matthean Community*, 96–109.
63. Altogether Luke omits Mark 6:45—8:26, 32–33, 37, 38b; 9:11–16, 21–25.
64. Johnson, *The Gospel of Luke*, 154.
65. Moessner, *Lord of the Banquet*.

voice that will follow in Luke's Travel Narrative. However, Moessner fails to correctly recognize the position of the Transfiguration in the larger rhetorical transition from Luke 5–18. Moessner is correct to note that before the mountaintop experience, Jesus is involved in discipleship training and after the descent Jesus is correcting the misunderstandings of the Twelve. However, in order to show the parallels with the canonical Exodus story, Moessner observes a very rigid literary structure in Luke 9:1–50 that seems rather forced.[66] What is more helpful is to view the Transfiguration as further defining the new leadership style of Jesus' followers worked out in the surrounding mission contexts (9:1–10 and 10:1–20).

In his article, Thomas W. Martin has observed how the Lukan Transfiguration is not focused exclusively on future triumphalism (as the majority of historical-critical studies suggest),[67] but rather centers on the humility of discipleship.[68] Through this rhetorical arrangement, Luke demonstrates how humility is an integral part of triumph's presence.[69] The two are tightly bound in Jesus' mind, and this understanding is necessary for the universal mission in which the Twelve will embark.

After the Twelve hear of Jesus' true identity at the mount of Transfiguration, Luke notes that they still fail to understand the nature of leadership that Jesus is advocating.[70] While Jesus is talking about being handed over to human powers, the Twelve are arguing about their leadership rank. As a result, Jesus takes a child as an illustration that their power does not come from themselves, but rather from the mission they are embarking on and who they represent in the process. As Jesus talks of this child, he is implying that He could choose anyone to do this task. This powerful illustration marks the true nature of this new leadership structure as the narrative moves on toward a more active role of the disciples. This lesson is compounded by John's response, as he complains of someone casting out demons who is not from their group (9:49). This echoes the complaint made by Joshua to Moses in Num 11:26–30, when men in the Israelite camp began prophesying in the Spirit even though they had not received formal

---

66. Ibid., 70

67. For the traditional historical-critical understanding of the Transfiguration as a foreshadowing of future glory, see Nolland, *Luke*, 497.

68. Martin, "What Makes Glory Glorious?," 3–26.

69. Ibid., 24.

70. Cf. Jesus' words to his disciples at the Last Supper regarding the nature of leadership (Luke 22:24–27).

The Transition from Jesus to His Disciples

approval from Moses. Moses' response to Joshua is telling, "Would that all the Lord's people were prophets, that the Lord would put His Spirit upon them!" If Luke has thus far characterized Jesus as the prophet like Moses,[71] it would stand to reason that Luke has intentionally alluded to this scene to demonstrate that Jesus is desiring to release power to many instead of limit it to a prestigious few.

Following the Commissioning of the Twelve and the Seventy-Two, Luke continues to develop the idea of an expanded pool of disciples through his inclusion of women into Jesus' ministry. In Luke 10:38–42, the author carefully inserts a passage about Mary and Martha to drive home the point that women will have a more expanded role in God's Kingdom than previously recognized in the Jewish subculture. Witherington notes the traditional role of women at this time: "A woman's sphere of influence or importance in the legal sense was confined to her connection to her family, her faithfulness to her husband, and her domestic responsibilities."[72] Jesus is actively expanding this familial boundary to include the work of his Kingdom.

In this short but significant passage, Luke highlights how women were afforded the opportunity to become full disciples of Jesus. Previously in his narrative, Luke has already taken several opportunities to describe the important place of women in Jesus' ministry, most notably the list of women traveling with Jesus in Luke 8:1–3.[73] Here, Luke strategically places this story to emphasize the new place of women among the disciples of Jesus. Jesus defends Mary's right to learn from him, and in the process Luke highlights how all women now have this privilege.

While Luke has used the material in 9:1—10:42 to demonstrate the transition of power from Jesus to his disciples, the Central Section (Luke 11–18) that follows will focus even more extensively on the type of leadership Jesus demands of his disciples. In order to demonstrate this new leadership style that has emerged, Luke purposefully takes the next eight chapters to juxtapose Jesus' disciples with current Jewish leadership. The result solidifies the continuity between Jesus and the unorthodox group of disciples he has chosen to lead the early church.

---

71. Johnson, *The Gospel*, 162, notes that Jesus' characterization as a prophet is intensified in the Central Section.

72. Witherington, *Women*, 2.

73. Ibid., 116–17.

Luke's Legato Historiography

This so-called "Central Section" of Luke has often puzzled biblical scholars, who have attempted to make sense of its unique literary structure. The apparent disorganization of these chapters has led the majority of scholars to view this Central Section as simply a convenient location for a variety of Jesus sayings. This leads to an unsatisfactory presentation of this section as haphazard, which does not align with Luke's overarching goal "to write an orderly narrative" (Luke 1:1–3). Unfortunately, those who have sought to find organization in these chapters have often forced *modern* organizational techniques onto the text. A better approach is to examine this Travel Narrative as the conclusion to an elaborate rhetorical transition designed by Luke to persuade his audience that the Twelve and the Seventy(-two) are legitimate successors to Jesus' ministry.

This Central Section consists almost exclusively of Jesus' teachings, although Jesus does perform some wonders (an exorcism in 14:1–6; the healing of a bent woman in 13:10–13; the man with dropsy in 14:1–6; the ten lepers in 17:11–19, and the blind man in 18:35–43). Johnson notes how Jesus addresses three carefully distinguished groups in his teachings: 1) the disciples who increasingly emerge as significant hearers of the word;[74] 2) "the crowd"[75]; and 3) Pharisees and lawyers. Johnson observes that the alternation of these various audiences creates tension.[76] However, it is not enough to say that Luke creates narrative tension. His fuller purpose is to draw a sharp distinction between the current leadership structures of his day and the type of leadership he is developing with his disciples. The content of this section has been carefully selected to reshape the memories of its first-century audience. As demonstrated earlier, the church at the time of Luke's Gospel had uncertainty surrounding the transition of power from the religious elites to everyday followers of Jesus. For Luke's audience, the dramatic shift in the hierarchy of God's people would have presented sizeable mental gaps in the continuity of recent history. Luke recognized these discontinuous staccato memories and responded by bridging the past together through a specific rhetorical arrangement. Luke's Central Section, therefore, is not simply a random assortment of unrelated material, but rather a deliberate juxtaposition of leadership styles.

74. The term μαθητης occurs more frequently in these nine chapters than anywhere else in the Gospel and eight times the expression "Jesus said to his disciples" is used followed by a body of teaching.

75. The term ὄχλος is used eighteen times in these nine chapters, while the term "people" (λαος) is used only three times.

76. Johnson, *The Gospel*, 164.

Conclusion

As in the last chapter, it has been shown again how Luke has developed a unique commemoration of past figures in history. In the time surrounding Luke's Gospel, multiple traditions existed surrounding Jesus and his eventual successors. It was demonstrated that at the end of the first century, certain confusion remained concerning the selection of Jesus' successors, and various solutions were offered by Luke's contemporaries. However, Luke has developed the most sophisticated arrangement of these ancient artifacts in his elaborate rhetorical transition spanning the middle half of his narrative.

The Lukan Jesus moves power away from current leadership structures of his day (including Pharisees, chief priests, etc.) primarily toward twelve unlikely successors. However, unlike previous traditions, Luke greatly expands his commemoration of the Twelve Apostles. Instead of limiting Jesus' successors to the Twelve, Luke spends considerable time expanding Jesus' followers to include the Seventy-two and also women. This unique commemoration also includes an elaborate journey with his followers (Luke 9–18) to contrast proper and improper leadership styles. This newly-developed leadership structure foreshadows the diverse leadership of the early church as described in the book of Acts.

It is further suggested in this chapter that the best explanation for Luke's unique rhetorical structure was to provide assurance to his audience(s) that no gaps existed between Jesus and his successors. Social memory theory demonstrates that gaps in leadership succession can provide significant identity struggles within a particular community. As a result, Luke provides reassurance of the continuity between Jesus and his successors through the use of an elaborate rhetorical transition stretching from Jesus' Galilean ministry (Luke 5–8) to the Travel Narrative (Luke 9–18). By anticipating the replacement of the traditional Jewish hierarchy with the Twelve in the middle of Jesus' Galilean ministry, Luke offers his audience time to assimilate these past remembrances.

As the transition moves more toward the integrated mission of the Twelve and the Seventy-Two, Jesus spends considerable time demonstrating how his chosen disciples will replace the previous Jewish regime. The Lukan Jesus, portrayed as a prophet like Moses with an authoritative voice, offers many new distinct characteristics for his successors. First, the focus of this new leadership style is on outward expansion rather than an inward, centrifugal mission. Second, the Lukan Jesus redefines purity boundaries, steering his successors toward a mission focused on the socially marginalized. Third, the Lukan Jesus authoritatively speaks of seeking God as one's sole provision. Fourth, this same Jesus models a leadership style focused on servanthood and humility. Through this lengthy Central Section of his Gospel, Luke offers his audience(s) a lengthy amount of time to accept this expanded presentation of the past. Luke has commemorated past artifacts in fresh ways because of the contemporary needs of his late first-century audience(s).

5

The Transition from Jesus to the Holy Spirit

AT THE END OF the first century, the early church struggled to fully comprehend the continuity between the person of Jesus and the person of the Holy Spirit. Where did Jesus' ministry end and that of the Holy Spirit begin? How did Jesus' death and resurrection factor into this transition? Why did the coming of the Holy Spirit seemingly transform Jesus' disciples into power-filled witnesses? Luke understood these mental discontinuities of the church and attempts to bridge these gaps with an elaborate rhetorical transition connecting the two volumes of his historiography. Through a careful interweaving of the ascension of Jesus with the full outpouring of the Holy Spirit, Luke highlights the continuity of salvation history at this important juncture in the early church.

This chapter will begin with an examination of the confusion surrounding the transition from Jesus to the Holy Spirit at the end of the first century and beginning of the second century. It will be demonstrated that these significant questions disrupted the identity of the church at the end of the first century. This will be followed by a specific look at how Luke has addressed these mental discontinuities through his legato narrative in Luke 24—Acts 2.

The Holy Spirit Remembered in Tradition

In order to discover how the Holy Spirit was remembered in the first and second century, it will be helpful to begin with an examination of the canonical gospels. The earlier Gospel of Mark offers little explicit information about the Holy Spirit in comparison with the Gospels of Matthew, Luke and John. Mark speaks of the Spirit primarily in the introduction of Jesus at his baptism by JBap (1:8, 10, 12), and then only rarely throughout the Gospel (3:29 in reference to exorcism and also in reference to prophetic inspiration at 12:36 and 13:11).[1]

Matthew's Gospel expands the terse Markan references to the Holy Spirit and adds some unique pneumatology of its own. This gospel demonstrates how the Spirit defines Jesus' mission as God's servant rather than Satan's.[2] There seems to be a large focus on defending Jesus against charges of sorcery and magic, and instead this gospel writer highlights how the Spirit empowers Jesus during his ministry (4:1). Matthew's Gospel attempts to highlight how the Holy Spirit connects Jesus to the Father, while at the same time denouncing heresy that Jesus was somehow possessed by an evil "spirit."

The Gospel of John offers an even more developed pneumatology than its Markan and Matthean predecessors, primarily during Jesus' Farewell Discourse (John 14–17). The Fourth Gospel writer makes clear that the Spirit will not arrive until Jesus leaves this earth (7:39; 16:7), highlighting the specific chronology for the audience. After Jesus' resurrection, he appears to his disciples and breathes the Holy Spirit on them (20:23). It would appear that the author of the Fourth Gospel is attempting to explain the relationship between Jesus and the Holy Spirit.

An examination of extrabiblical literature makes clear that some effort existed outside the New Testament context to clarify the links between Jesus and the Holy Spirit. *First Clement* 42:1–4 speaks of the unity between the resurrected Lord Jesus Christ and the Holy Spirit, as both empowered the apostles for their ministry. It reads, Παραγγελίας οὖν λαβόντες καὶ πληροφορηθέντες . . . ἐν τῷ λόγῳ τοῦ θεοῦ μετὰ πληροφορίας πνεύματος ἁγίου ἐξῆλθον εὐαγγελιζόμενοι τὴν βασιλείαν τοῦ θεοῦ μέλλειν ἔρχεσθαι. This text goes on to mention how the apostles appointed bishops and deacons through the testing of the Spirit. This emphasis on the desired continuity between Jesus' earthly ministry and his followers likely stems from certain heresies that demanded that the church show a continuous succession of God's people.[3] Likewise, *2 Clement* 14:4 equates the Spirit and Christ. At one point, in an attempt to demonstrate the importance of the

---

1. This lack of attention to the Spirit seems to have led Luke to better clarify the relationship between Jesus and the Spirit. Although, see Mansfield, *Spirit*, 38–39.

2. Keener, *The Spirit*, 117.

3. *1 Clem.* 1:1. See also *1 Clem.* 46:5–6 which speak about schisms and the need to recognize we have one God and one Christ and one Spirit.

flesh for the church, it says εἰ Χριστός, ὁ κύριος ὁ σώσας ἡμᾶς, ὢν μὲν τὸ πρῶτον πνεῦμα, ἐγένετο σὰρξ καὶ οὕτως ἡμᾶς ἐκάλεσεν· οὕτως καὶ ἡμεῖς ἐν ταύτῃ τῇ σαρκὶ ἀποληψόμεθα τὸν μισθόν.[4]

Ascension of Isaiah is a Christian document written in the late first century or early second century. It demonstrates the paradoxical effort to distinguish Jesus from the Holy Spirit while also highlighting the unity between the two. As the seer "Isaiah" joins the angels in praising in the sixth heaven, he worships the "primal Father, and the Beloved One [Jesus] and the Holy Spirit" (8:18). Both Jesus and the Holy Spirit occupy a place on the side the Father's divine throne, and both worship the Father together (9:35). While there are these similarities, the text is clear to distinguish the Holy Spirit from Christ and God. The Spirit is the only one to be designated as an "angel," usually in the phrase "angel of the Holy Spirit" (7:23; 8:14; 9:35-36, 39-40; 10:4; 11:4, 33). Loren T. Stuckenbruck poses the questions: "What accounts for the worthiness of the Spirit to be worshipped alongside God, and why is the Spirit nonetheless apparently assigned to a subordinate position, a position lower than that of Christ?"[5] The Ascension of Isaiah demonstrates an early sign of Trinitarian worship in Christian contexts. It would appear that the author is attempting to make a place for the Holy Spirit to be worshipped, as an extension of the binitarian praise that had become characteristic of the Christian faith.[6]

Justin Martyr speaks of the Spirit as well in the mid second century, though rarely moving beyond the pneumatology of the NT.[7] He chooses not to sharply differentiate between Christ and the Holy Spirit, showing that even into the second century there was significant overlap between Jesus and the Holy Spirit. For example, at one point Justin states, "Thus the Spirit and the Power from God cannot be understood as anything else than the Word (τὸν λόγον), who is also the first-begotten of God" (*1 Apol.* 33:6-9). While there is some overlap between the figures of Jesus Christ and the Spirit, Justin also draws a distinction between the two. In *1 Apology* 13,

---

4. *2 Clem.* 9.5.

5. Stuckenbruck, "The Holy Spirit," 310.

6 For information on binitarian devotion as unique in Jewish circles, see Hurtado, *Lord Jesus Christ*, 27-63.

7. It is of interest that Justin's favorite term for the Spirit is "the Prophetic Spirit." It is found 25 times in *Apologies* (1 *Apol.* 6.2; 13.3; 31.1; 32.2; 33.2, 5; 35.3; 38.1; 39.1; 40.1, 5; 41.1; 42.1; 44.1, 11; 47.1; 48.4; 51.1; 53.4, 6; 59.1; 60.8; 63.2, 12, 14) and 12 times in *Dialogue with Trypho* (32.3; 38.2; 43.3, 4; 49.6; 53.4; 55.1; 56.5; 77.3; 84.2; 91.4; 139.1).

Justin states that Christ is "in second place to the true God himself" (13:3; cf 12:7), and the prophetic Spirit is "in the third rank."

Once, when asked by Trypho how Christ can be pre-existent God and also become incarnate and be filled with the Spirit, as if he lacked this before (citing Isaiah 11:1ff.), Justin responds in a way that admits the complexity of the issue and discusses the chronology of various eras of history:

> You have inquired most discreetly and most prudently, for truly there does seem to be a difficulty; but listen to what I say, that you may perceive the reason of this also. The Scripture says that these enumerated powers of the Spirit have come on Him, not because He stood in need of them, but because they would rest in Him, i.e., would find their accomplishment in Him, so that there would be no more prophets in your nation after the ancient custom: and this fact you plainly perceive. For after Him no prophet has arisen among you.... He rested, i.e., ceased, when *He* came, after whom, in the times of this dispensation wrought out by Him amongst men, it was requisite that such gifts should cease from you; and having received their rest in Him, should again, as had been predicted, become gifts which, from the grace of His Spirit's power, He imparts to those who believe in Him, according as He deems each man worthy thereof. I have already said, and do again say, that it had been prophesied that this would be done by Him after His ascension to heaven. It is accordingly said, 'He ascended on high, He led captivity captive, He gave gifts unto the sons of men.' And again, in another prophecy it is said: 'And it shall come to pass after this, I will pour out My Spirit on all flesh, and on My servants, and on My handmaids, and they shall prophesy.[8]

Graham N. Stanton notes that this citation highlights the Holy Spirit's chronological position in relation to Christ, rather than one of subordination, although he admits there may be a hint of the latter here as well.[9]

Justin notes that Christians are charged with madness for giving to "a crucified man second place after the unchangeable and eternal God, begetter of all things" (1 *Apol.* 13:4). Justin feels the need to then defend the person of Jesus Christ. However, it is apparently more acceptable to hold the Holy Spirit in high regard in the third place and no defense is needed. What is notable in the work by Justin is the effort to show the rational continuity

---

8. *Dial.* 87.
9. Stanton, "The Spirit," 330.

of God's work throughout history, from the prophets of the OT to Jesus to the Holy Spirit working through Jesus' followers.

It has been briefly highlighted that the early church struggled to fully understand the continuity between Jesus and the Holy Spirit through the first century and into the second century. Questions existed regarding the relationship between Jesus and the Holy Spirit, and various solutions were offered. Luke apparently felt that no previous record of the transition from Jesus to the Holy Spirit was adequate, prompting him to develop a legato narrative of events. The rest of this chapter will focus on Luke's answer to the questions surrounding the Holy Spirit.

Lukan Remembrances of Jesus and the Holy Spirit

While traditional studies on Lukan pneumatology have focused the majority of their efforts on how Luke follows Paul in attributing soteriological significance to the gift of the Holy Spirit,[10] more recent studies have moved the conversation beyond this basic dichotomy of a "Spirit of Prophecy" versus a "Spirit of Sonship."[11] While significant research has been accomplished in this field, a couple gaps in scholarship still remain, which this chapter aims to remedy. First, it is surprising how many recent studies apply a rigid epochal schema to Luke-Acts. By developing an artificial divide between Luke's Gospel and Acts, one risks missing the interweaving of these volumes to demonstrate a continuous salvation history. Second, it is notable that very few studies have thoroughly examined how the larger rhetorical arrangement of Luke-Acts influences the presentation of the Holy Spirit. It would appear that this is the result of a lack of attention paid to the genre of Luke-Acts when studying pneumatology, as studies

10. In 1888, Hermann Gunkel established the first major study on Lukan pneumatology in which he drew a distinction between Luke and Paul. Gunkel, *Die Wirkungen*, 18–19, 42–43. In 1926, Friedrich Büchsel produced a work in response that emphasized the continuity between the Lukan and Pauline notions of the Holy Spirit. Büchsel, *Der Geist Gottes*. Writing shortly after Büchsel, von Baer attempted a mediating position between Gunkel and Büchsel. Von Baer is mostly remembered for his three-epoch schema of Lukan *heilsgeschichte*, a paradigm embraced by Conzelmann in later years. Baer, *Der Heilige Geist*.

11. Some notable studies on Lukan pneumatology include the following: Dunn, *Baptism*; Haya-Prats, *Empowered Believer*; Menzies, *The Development*; Turner, *Power*; Kuecker, *The Spirit*; Wenk, *Community-Forming Power*. For a summary of past scholarship on Pauline pneumatology, see Vos, *Traditionsgeschichtliche*, 1–25.

of the Spirit have traditionally focused on the historical development of pneumatology in the early church. Through an examination of how Luke rhetorically shapes his historiography, a fuller understanding of Lukan pneumatology will result. It will be demonstrated directly below how Luke desires to highlight the continuity between Jesus' earthly ministry and the Spirit-empowered ministry of his followers, and how he shapes his rhetorical narrative accordingly.

Similar to the Lukan rhetorical transitions examined in the previous two chapters, here at the seam of his two volumes Luke also connects his narrative using the "chain-link" technique. The following rhetorical structure can be observed in Luke 24—Acts 2:

A	The Resurrected Jesus	Luke 24:1–53
b	Foreshadow of the Holy Spirit	Luke 24:47–49
a	Retrospective Look at the Resurrected Jesus	Luke 24:50—Acts 1:12
B	The Coming of the Holy Spirit	Acts 1:1–2:47ff

This A-b-a/a-B structure ties the resurrected Jesus with the coming of the Holy Spirit. As will be observed below, the primary content that overlaps between Luke and Acts is the recounting of Jesus' ascension and the gift of the promised Holy Spirit, and it is here where some confusion would have likely existed among the church of Luke's day. Each section of this rhetorical transition will now be examined in order to demonstrate how foreshadowing and retrospective elements persuade Luke's audience to tightly connect these past events in their minds.

The Resurrected Jesus (Luke 24:1–53)

While the chain-link transition at the seam of Luke-Acts serves to bind the entire work together, this chapter will focus specific attention on the overlap of material between Luke 24 and Acts 2. Luke is careful to highlight the Holy Spirit in the earthly life of Jesus. This Spirit is spoken of during his birth (Luke 1:35) and at the inception of Jesus' adult ministry (3:16, 22; 4:14, 18). At a very early stage in his narrative, Luke begins to prepare his audience for the transition to the Holy Spirit, but the focus of this first of Luke's two volumes is on the person Jesus and his work in Israel.

Throughout Jesus' ministry, he made it clear that it was necessary for him to suffer, die, and rise again (9:21, 44). While his ministry focused on εὐαγγελίσασθαι πτωχοῖς (4:18), it becomes increasingly clear throughout

The Transition from Jesus to the Holy Spirit

the narrative that his life would be threatened. For a primarily Gentile audience, it is understandable that they would struggle with the unusual traditions surrounding Jesus' resurrection and ascension. As N.T. Wright has shown at length in *The Resurrection of the Son of God*, corporeal resurrection was a foreign concept to Greeks, and for Jews resurrection was mainly spoken of as an eschatological event for the entire nation.[12] A bodily resurrection for a single individual like Jesus would have required clarification, and Luke has chosen to make it very clear in this transitional section that the earthly Jesus is similar to the resurrected and ascended Jesus. Green states, "On the one hand, then, the narrative rules out any notion of the resuscitation of a corpse; on the other, it excludes interpretations of the resurrection as merely an ethereal event. Luke's narrative affirms a resurrected Jesus over against these other options for the afterlife current in the Hellenistic world."[13] In Luke 24:36–43, multiple proofs are given to emphasize the continuity of Jesus' physical body, such as allowing the Eleven to touch his hands and feet, and eating a meal.[14]

It is important to note the significance of Jesus' words in 24:39, πνεῦμα σάρκα καὶ ὀστέα οὐκ ἔχει καθὼς ἐμὲ θεωρεῖτε ἔχοντα. This is the only mention of the word πνευμα in the final chapter of Luke's Gospel, and Jesus directly states that he is not a spirit at this point. It would seem that at the end of the first century there were many in the church who struggled to draw a distinction between Jesus' resurrected body and the Holy Spirit. Perhaps, this is why Luke specifies that the resurrected Jesus was with the Eleven for forty long days. In Acts 1:3–4, Luke seems to emphasize that this is Jesus as a person and not yet the Holy Spirit, since he is eating with the disciples again (like in Luke 24:42), and he is offering many convincing proofs (as in 24:28–42).

In the final chapter of his Gospel, Luke demonstrates that while Jesus' form is different, he is still the same person found throughout the Third Gospel. Johnson notes how the scene on the road to Emaus compliments the scene of Jesus' appearance to his disciples. The first shows a Jesus who could appear as a stranger without being recognized, while the second emphasizes the other side: he is not a ghost but a real person and Jesus states,

---

12. Wright, *The Resurrection*. Although, see Daniel 12:1–3, where it appears that two groups of resurrection are mentioned.

13. Green, *The Gospel*, 852.

14. Keener, *Acts*, 666. This Lukan language of "many proofs" was common in Hellenistic historiography and used in courtroom settings as irrefutable.

"It is I myself!"[15] Throughout Luke 24, Jesus speaks words that he spoke to his disciples prior to his crucifixion, highlighting the continuity of his message before and after his resurrection.

It should be noted that even as Luke's Gospel nears its conclusion, the disciples still do not have a full understanding of Jesus' significance. Even in Luke 24:36ff., the Eleven still react with fear and terror at the risen Jesus (24:41 notes their disbelief), and it is only through the mediation of Jesus that their minds are opened to understand the Scriptures. Luke is careful to note here the shortcomings of Jesus' followers, and this fear will be quickly replaced by power and boldness once the Holy Spirit enters the narrative in Acts 2. After his resurrection, Jesus interprets the Scriptures to many (the two on the road; 24:26–27 and the Eleven in 24:44–47). It will be through the Holy Spirit that the Apostles will be able to interpret the Scriptures through the new fresh lens of Jesus' life, death, and resurrection.[16]

Foreshadow of the Holy Spirit (Luke 24:47–49)

Before concluding his Gospel with the ascension of Jesus, Luke briefly foreshadows the next phase in salvation history. These three short verses are packed full of significant themes that will be fully narrated in the book of Acts. This section creates an anticipation on the part of the listening audience. The disciples have already begun to splinter apart (note the two already leaving for Emmaus in 24:13). Will the disciples remain at Jerusalem? Will they receive power from on high for their mission?

The transition from Jesus' earthly presence to his ascension is highly significant in the Lukan narrative. This Spirit-empowered Jesus is ascending to heaven, threatening the very experience of salvation that Luke has described as commencing in his Gospel.[17] It is as if Luke expects his listeners to ask, "What will now happen to the community of believers?" Conzelmann had developed a bleak picture of the church after Jesus ascended, but this has been largely refuted. Bovon rightly states that for Luke the period of the church is not just an uncomfortable waiting room, where the church can recall portraits of Jesus, who spoke about the coming Kingdom of

---

15. Johnson, *The Gospel*, 405.

16. Ibid. The OT also helped the early church in understanding their role as witness to these events, which is described by the following: Evans and Sanders, *Luke and Scripture*, 14–15; Songer, "Isaiah," 459–70; Flamming, "The New Testament," 89–103.

17. Turner, *Power*, 346.

The Transition from Jesus to the Holy Spirit

God which is slow to arrive.[18] Rather for Luke, there is no gap in salvation history at this point. The Kingdom of God which Jesus inaugurated during his earthly ministry is continued through the same Holy Spirit who empowered his ministry. Johnson states, "The promise of the Holy Spirit is the final statement of Jesus in the Gospel, and is followed immediately by this first account of his ascension. For Luke, these are two moments of the same process: the 'withdrawal' of Jesus is not so much an absence as it is a presence in a new and more powerful mode: when Jesus is not among them as another specific body, he is accessible to all as life-giving Spirit."[19] Turner states, "The key transitional passages (Lk. 24.47–49 and Acts 1.1–8) mention only one power that Jesus will give from the Father that could possibly be expected to continue the saving/transforming momentum of Jesus' ministry, and that is the Holy Spirit."[20] What Jesus began, the Holy Spirit will seamlessly continue, and Luke utilizes this passage to bind these stages of salvation history together. Specifically, Luke linguistically connects this passage with the beginning of Acts through some key terms (δυναμιν in Luke 24:49 and Acts 1:8; also μαρτυρες in Luke 24:48 and Acts 1:8).[21]

Through Jesus speaking words about the promised Holy Spirit prior to his ascension, Luke has woven their stories together, foreshadowing what is to come in the second volume of his historiography. Though the Holy Spirit is not directly mentioned in Luke 24, the book of Acts makes clear that "the promise" referred to in Luke 24:49 is the same Holy Spirit promised in Acts 1:4–5; 2:33, 38–39. Turner notes that Luke's listeners should, therefore, not be surprised that the Spirit of prophecy in the upcoming book of Acts will bring salvation to Israel since they would have already seen the Spirit's work of salvation powerfully manifested through Jesus during his ministry. Thus, the pouring out of the Holy Spirit on the disciples at Pentecost would only serve to further deepen the Holy Spirit's salvific work and extend it to others. Turner states, "The transitional passages (especially Acts 1.1–8) would strongly suggest to the reader that it is the gift of the Spirit to Israel that provides the ongoing self-manifesting and transforming presence of God in strength, and so the gift of the Spirit which lies at the heart of the hope for Israel's ongoing salvation/transformation and her mission as the

---

18. Bovon, *Luke*, 27.
19. Johnson, *The Gospel*, 405.
20. Turner, *Power*, 347.
21. Tannehill states that "witness" is the key point of transition between Luke's two volumes. Tannehill, *Narrative Unity*, 1:294.

Isaianic servant and light to the nations."²² The salvation of Israel will continue through the Holy Spirit's empowerment of Jesus' disciples.

Retrospective Look at the Resurrected Jesus (Luke 24:50—Acts 1:12)

After foreshadowing the powerful work of the Holy Spirit in 24:47-49, Luke returns his attention to the earthly ministry of Jesus and his ascension. This "pause" helps Luke's listening audience to tightly connect the work of Jesus with the work of the Holy Spirit. Since the time of Henry Cadbury in the early twentieth century, the majority of biblical scholars have read Luke and Acts together as a unified historical writing of some type.²³ However, the continuity between Luke's two volumes has been challenged in recent decades. Richard Pervo has revived a second-century date for the composition of Acts, and in the process called for the separation of Acts from Luke's Gospel.²⁴ While Pervo has attracted a modest following of scholars toward the separation of Luke and Acts, the majority of scholars still affirm the authorial and compositional unity of Luke and Acts.²⁵ In this section, this continuity between Luke and Acts will be observed through the deliberate rhetorical connections created by the author.

It was customary in antiquity to connect various volumes through certain rhetorical techniques. Parsons notes that sequential books in antiquity employed prologues in one of three ways: (1) summary of preceding book and outline of what was covered in present volume (Polybius, *Hist.* 2.1.4–8; 3.1.5–3.3; see also explanatory note in the fragments of book 11; Diodorus Siculus, *Library of History* 1.4.6–5.1; Philo, *Mos.* 2.1); (2) retrospective summary of preceding book and move directly into the contents of the present work (Xenophon, *Anab.*; Josephus, *Ant.*; Herodian, *Hist.*); (3) prospective summary, but do not mention previous volume (Appian, *Hist. Rom.* 1.13-15; Diodorus Siculus, *Library of History* 2.1; Eusebius, *Hist. eccl.* 7). Parsons notes that Luke followed the first pattern.²⁶ While Luke does

---

22. Turner, *Power*, 347.

23. Cadbury, *The Making of Luke-Acts*, 8–10.

24. Parsons and Pervo, *Rethinking*. See also Gregory and Rowe, *The Reception* and Gregory, *Rethinking*.

25. For various types of "unity" between Luke and Acts, see Witherington, *Acts*, 5. Also, see Trocme, *Le "Livre des Acts."*

26. Parsons, *Acts*, 26.

The Transition from Jesus to the Holy Spirit

implement this ancient convention, it becomes clear that this bridging is not merely ornamental. Rather, he spends an abundance of effort to weave together the traditions of Jesus and the Holy Spirit and in the process strongly communicates the continuity between Jesus' earthly ministry and the work of the Holy Spirit that follows in salvation history. Regarding the specific interweaving of Luke 24 and Acts 1, Johnson states, "Luke could hardly have provided the reader with a clearer indication of how he wanted the two volumes to be read together as mutually interpretive."[27]

In the ascension accounts in Luke's Gospel and Acts, the author includes many elements common to Greco-Roman (and Jewish) assumption stories.[28] Despite some variations in the two ascension accounts, the differences can be explained by separate literary agendas at the end of the Gospel and the beginning of Acts. Witherington states, "In Luke 24 the account serves as a means of closing the first volume, but in Acts 1 the story of the ascension and final instructions serves to initiate what follows."[29] Maddox notes that rather than divide these two volumes, the ascension accounts serve as a major bridge from one to the other. He states, "The ascension is for Luke the point of intersection of Christology, eschatology and ecclesiology."[30] Green notes that the ascension of Jesus functions in at least two ways: (1) Luke draws a connection between the going of Jesus and the coming of the Spirit and (2) Luke addresses the problem of continuity in God's salvation-historical design.[31]

This connection between Jesus and the Spirit can be observed through Jesus' interaction with the Apostles. At the end of his Gospel, Luke demonstrates that the Eleven have finally become credible witnesses of Jesus' identity. Throughout Luke 24, the attitudes of the Eleven significantly progress (beginning with perplexity in v. 4 and ending in continual worship of God

---

27. Johnson, *The Gospel*, 405.

28. As noted by Parsons, (1) a mountain as the site of the assumption (Lucian, *Hermot.* 7; Apollodorus, *Bibl.* 2.7.7; Minucius Felix, *Oct.* 22.7; Diodorus Siculus, *Library of History* 3.60.3; Aurelius Victor, *Vir. Illustr.* 2.13; see Acts 1:12); (2) clouds are typical elements (Apollodorus, *Bibl.* 2.7.7; Dionysius of Halicarnassus, *Ant. Rom.* 1.77.2; Plutarch, *Num.* 2.23 in *Lives*; *T. Ab.* 8.3; 10.2; 12.1,9; 4 *Ezra* 5.7; see Acts 1:9); (3) appearances by the ascended one is also a common motif (Plutarch, *Rom.* 28.13; Livy, *History of Rome* 1.16.58; Ovid, *Fasti* 2.499–509; Lucian, *Peregr.* 40; Philostratus, *Life of Apollonius of Tyana* 8.31). There are also some similarities in Elijah's ascension story in 2 Kings 4. Parsons, *Acts*, 27.

29. Witherington, *Acts*, 107. See also Parsons, *The Departure*, 190, 194.

30. Maddox, *The Purpose*, 10.

31. Green, *The Gospel*, 862. See also Korn, *Die Geschichte Jesu*, 175–89.

in v. 53).³² Likewise, Jesus opens the minds of the disciples to understand the Scriptures. In this way, Luke has not only highlighted the transition from Jesus to the Eleven, but has also inscribed the story of the early church into both his own story and that of the Israelite Scriptures.³³ Acts 1:2 specifically notes that the apostles were "chosen" by Jesus, and then proceeds to highlight the lengthy amount of time the Eleven spent with the resurrected Jesus before his ascension. The fact that the apostles spent forty days with the resurrected Jesus receiving clarification about the Kingdom of God would have reassured Luke's audience of the continuity between Jesus and the Spirit-inspired Eleven.³⁴ Further, this forty-day period of preparation reminds Luke's audience of Jesus' forty-day preparation for his own ministry in Luke's Gospel.³⁵ Jesus offers to the apostles the same Holy Spirit who empowered his own ministry (Acts 1:8; cf. Luke 3).³⁶ Therefore, despite the differences in demographic focus between Jesus and his disciples, the same Holy Spirit has anointed both of them for their work.

Luke takes the opportunity at the beginning of Acts for Jesus himself to introduce the coming Holy Spirit. In Acts 1:4, while Luke is summarizing Jesus' earthly ministry, Jesus interrupts this narrator to break into the scene directly.³⁷ "All that Jesus began to do and to teach" in the first volume is continuing here even in the first few verses of Acts, showing the continuity of Jesus' ministry in both volumes. This narrative would have reassured its first audiences, demonstrating that the Jesus described in Luke's Gospel is the same Jesus who is now exalted with God. Raymond Brown notes "It is Jesus himself who gives the outline of the book of Acts (1:8); Luke might have done this himself in the prologue to Acts, but by having Jesus do it, Luke shows the continuity between the Church and Jesus."³⁸ This is a Jesus with a consistent message for Luke's audiences at the end of the first century.

---

32. Schubert, "The Structure," 165–86.

33. Green, *The Theology*, 856.

34. Parsons notes the popular ancient convention of listing successors of certain major historical figures. Parsons, *Acts*, 30.

35. Keener, *Acts*, 670.

36. Johnson notes the OT parallels of Moses and Elijah; the Spirit was transmitted from both to their successor at their departure (Deut 34:9; 2 Kgs 2:9-22). Johnson, *The Gospel*, 405. Keener also notes the parallels between Elijah/Elisha and Jesus/disciples. Keener, *Acts*, 711–13.

37. Moessner, "Triadic Synergy," 301.

38. Brown, *The Birth*, 242.

The Transition from Jesus to the Holy Spirit

J. B. Lightfoot offers some insightful thoughts regarding the purposeful interweaving of Luke and Acts at this juncture. He first notes that in Acts 1:1, through word order, Luke places prominence on the word ηρξατο. The first volume of Luke's historiography, therefore, was only about what Jesus *began* to do and to teach, not the full extent of his ministry. Rather, the work of Jesus will continue through the giving of the Holy Spirit described just verses later. Lightfoot moves on to describe the connectedness between the two ascension accounts given in Luke 24 and Acts 1. Lightfoot proceeds to note Jesus' continued role in the second volume of Luke's historiography. Prayer is offered to the Lord Jesus for guidance in the choosing of a twelfth apostle (1:24). It is Jesus himself who is described by Luke as pouring out the Holy Spirit (2:33). Jesus continues to perform miracles through his disciples' hands (4:10; 9:34). He is with Stephen at his death (7:55), and appears to Saul of Tarsus (9:5). Jesus even directs the travels of his disciples, forbidding them to go to Bithynia (16:7).[39] The ministry of Jesus in Luke's Gospel certainly continues seamlessly in the Book of Acts.

The Coming of the Holy Spirit (Acts 1:13—2:47ff)

Luke has already foreshadowed the coming Holy Spirit in Luke 24:49, and his listening audience would have anticipated this Spirit of God coming down from on high (ἐξ ὕψους). It is not surprising then, that the Eleven seem to expect this Spirit after Jesus is taken up to the sky in Acts 1:9–11. Having been corrected by the angelic figures in 1:10, they returned from the Mount of Olives to the upper room where they were staying in Jerusalem.[40] One might expect the immediate outpouring of the Holy Spirit, but Luke's narrative keeps the audience in suspense by describing the replacement of Judas Iscariot among the Twelve. Not only does this provide suspense, but it also allows for the continuation of Jesus' ministry to Israel, as the Apostles focus on the number Twelve again.[41]

It is not until The Day of Pentecost (2:1) that the promise from the Father arrives. This section of Luke's historiography has been heavily scrutinized, namely with regard to the question over whether Lukan

---

39. Lightfoot, *The Acts*, 71–72.

40. Parsons notes the literary device used in the rhetorical question (see Quintilian, *Inst.* 9.2.7), "Why are you standing staring at the sky?" (Parsons, *Acts*, 29).

41. For the alternate view that the disciples' actions to reestablish "the Twelve" highlights their continued ethnocentricity, see Kuecker, *The Spirit*, 107–10.

pneumatology has a salvific dimension or is exclusively portrayed as power for ministry.[42] However, what has been largely neglected in these studies is the rhetorical dimensions of this passage in Luke's larger narrative. Here Luke is not focused on an excursus of pneumatology, but rather to demonstrate the continuity that occurs at this epochal shift in salvation history.

It is important to note that Luke has intentionally structured this episode to parallel the inauguration of Jesus' ministry as found in Luke 3.[43] It therefore becomes obvious that Luke desires to connect Jesus' earthly ministry with the Spirit's empowering for ministry.[44] These parallel events present a conventional technique utilized by ancient historians to demonstrate a continuity in history. Trompf describes what Luke is attempting to accomplish:

> Luke was not interested in arranging his material as orderly *midrashim* or *pesherim* (commentary or interpretation) upon long sequences found in scriptures, nor was prophecy fulfillment for him only a way of authenticating Jesus or showing the ancient oracles to be right. Luke was fundamentally interested in more direct historical connections, as a historian of the Hellenistic period. He wrote as though established historical events, which for him were divinely guided, had their own inner relatedness, connections between events amounting to the virtual reenactment of special happenings . . . the main point is that he emerges as an historian comparable to Polybius (who, after all, managed to infuse a theological significance into his work), rather than as someone concerned to make a series of evangelistic and theological assertions in the form of a narrative.[45]

Max Turner has noted the various ways in which Luke has deliberately developed an analogy with Jesus' Jordan experience.[46] In both cases, individuals who already enjoy a committed relationship with God receive a prophetic endowment of the Holy Spirit during the context of prayer (Luke 3:21–22; Acts 2:1). The Holy Spirit offers both parties the empowering to proclaim the good news (Luke 4:18–21; 24:47–49; Acts 1:8; 2:11), and each

---

42. Dunn, *Baptism*, 41. Menzies, "Luke," 115–38.

43. Witherington, *Acts*, 128.

44. Possibly even beyond the parallels in Luke 3, Marguerat notes that Luke 12:49–50 foreshadows the fire and baptism that will come in Acts 2. Marguerat, *The First Christian Historian*, 51.

45. Trompf, *Idea*, 129. Concerning the idea of historical recurrence, see also Clare Rothschild, *Rhetoric*.

46. Turner, *Power*, 343–46.

The Transition from Jesus to the Holy Spirit

offers a sermon explaining the prophetic gift that has come on them (Luke 4:16; Acts 2:14–39).[47]

It is notable that the Holy Spirit functions in the early chapters of Acts to provide evidence that Jesus is Lord and Christ. This is not a distinct ministry, but the Spirit validates and witnesses to everything Jesus just accomplished in Luke's Gospel. He empowers the Twelve with signs and words to further spread the ministry of Jesus beyond Jerusalem. The events at Pentecost demonstrate the continuity between the work of Jesus and that of the Holy Spirit.[48] Luke has gone to great lengths to rhetorically bind this narrative representation of early Christianity together with the previous ministry of Jesus. The coming of the Spirit in Acts 2, therefore, should not present any major surprises to Luke's listening audience, as they have been prepared for this event by the last chapter of Luke's Gospel and the first chapter of Acts.

Following the coming of the Spirit upon the disciples, Peter offers a message describing the interrelationship between Jesus and the Holy Spirit. If Luke had not already made clear the relationship between the resurrected Jesus and the promised Holy Spirit, he will make certain of their connection in Peter's Pentecost sermon, which is twice as long as the Pentecost event itself.[49] He will examine OT prophets concerning the coming of the Holy Spirit as well as the crucified and raised Jesus. This sermon will then be concluded by a summary section of the Spirit-filled community of believers in Acts 2:43-47.

Acts 2:33 further tightens the links already established between Jesus and the Spirit. Peter states that Jesus received the promised Holy Spirit from the Father and he has poured (cf. 2:17, 18) this Spirit out on his followers. It is also notable that Peter goes on to say, "Let the entire house of Israel know (γινωσκέτω) with certainty (ἀσφαλῶς) that God has made him [Jesus] both Lord and Messiah, this Jesus whom you crucified" (2:36). This parallels Luke's preface (Luke 1:4), demonstrating that this is the type of transition that Luke is crafting to provide clarification for his listening audience. Luke's audiences are prompted to ask the same questions as those in the crowd at Pentecost, "What should we do?" Peter then ties together both Jesus and the Holy Spirit

---

47. These parallels between Jordan and Pentecost have long been recognized in biblical scholarship. See Baer, *Heilige Geist*, 85. More recently, see Menzies, *Development*, 201, 206–7.

48. Witherington correctly refutes some who claim that Luke invented the notion of the coming of the Spirit at Pentecost. Witherington, *Acts*, 130.

49. Parsons, *Acts*, 41.

in his response, further explaining how these two relate together after Jesus' ascension. The crowd is to receive forgiveness of sins through Jesus Christ and then one will receive the gift of the Holy Spirit, what God has promised.[50] The people are told to σώθητε ἀπὸ τῆς γενεᾶς (2:40) and later Luke narrates that ὁ δὲ κύριος προσετίθει τοὺς σῳζομένους (2:47). It is the Lord (Jesus) who is bringing salvation (cf. 2:21 where everyone who calls on the name of the Lord will be saved), and the Holy Spirit who follows bringing various charismatic and communal manifestations of his power.

Acts 2:43–47 explains the various manifestations of the Holy Spirit. Acts 2:43 goes on to mention that many wonders and signs were being performed through the apostles. Wenk states that "wonders and signs" in the OT are not only "attestation of a truth but the realization of salvation."[51] Kuecker notes, "Luke follows this tradition, using the phrase to describe action of God that breaks into human affairs to bring deliverance, healing, or salvation."[52] Kuecker also notes how Peter has modified the LXX version of Joel 3:3 to include the word σημεια (2:19), highlighting the idea of signs and wonders.[53] Again, in 2:22, Jesus is said to have done wonders and signs. Luke is creating an organic connection between Jesus doing wonders and signs (2:22) and the disciples doing wonders and signs (2:43). Using Peter's adjustment of Joel 3, Luke highlights that those who perform wonders and signs are empowered by the Holy Spirit as δοῦλοι or δοῦλαι of God.[54]

Conclusion

The mnemonic artifacts of Jesus and the Holy Spirit are commemorated in a variety of ways in the early church. This chapter has highlighted several of these particular remembrances both inside and outside the biblical canon. Existing traditions would have placed some boundaries on the range of presentations, since most communities would not accept a new narrative

---

50. Haya-Prats talks about forgiveness of sins coming from Jesus alone and not the Holy Spirit. The Holy Spirit is given to those who already have faith, not *for* faith. Similarly, Haya-Prats talks about God as the one who calls people to him. Haya-Prats, *Empowered Believers*, 187.

51. Wenk, *Community-Forming Power*, 251.

52. Kuecker, *The Spirit*, 133. He notes the following OT passages: Exodus 7:3, 11:9–10; Deut 4:34; 6:22; 7:19; 11:3; 26:8; 29:3; 34:11; Isaiah 8:18; Daniel 4:34.

53. Ibid., 132.

54. Ibid., 133.

The Transition from Jesus to the Holy Spirit

that completely deviated from the accepted traditions. Still, a variety of commemorative performances seemed to exist in the time period surrounding Luke-Acts.

These various remembrances of Jesus and the Holy Spirit seem to indicate that at times the first-century church struggled to see the full relationship between these two figures. It would appear that Luke was not completely satisfied with previous narrative attempts to connect Jesus and the Holy Spirit. Namely, Mark's Gospel lacks any overt attempt to develop the continuity between the two phases of early Christianity that these figures represent.

Unlike previous traditions, Luke-Acts contains an elaborate rhetorical transition to bridge the gap between Jesus and the Holy Spirit. It has been suggested in this chapter that the most logical explanation for such a rhetorical technique is Luke's desire to reassure his audience(s) of the continuity of salvation history at this important juncture in nascent Christianity. Ancient societies strongly desired to find continuity with the past, and Luke is structuring his historiography to facilitate this connectedness.

Luke's commemoration of Jesus and the Holy Spirit takes the form of a rhetorical transition and this is significant for several reasons. First, this important transition bridges together Luke's two volumes. As one who had a strong desire to produce a seamless account of salvation history, Luke would have placed much emphasis on the continuity between the two volumes of his historiography. Second, this transition bridges the work of Jesus found in the Gospels with the work of the Holy Spirit found in the book of Acts. Beginning early on in the Gospel, Luke foreshadows the work of the Holy Spirit in anticipation of the full outpouring in the book of Acts. Likewise, Jesus does not simply disappear once the book of Acts begins, but reappears at various junctures throughout Luke's second volume. Third, this transition further bridges Jesus' ministry with that of his many followers. The same Holy Spirit who descended on Jesus at his baptism (Luke 3) will also empower his followers throughout the book of Acts. Luke has clearly organized his narrative to weave these phases of early Christianity together, and social memory theory has assisted in understanding why.

6

The Transition from Peter to Paul

As has been suggested in the previous three chapters, the late first-century church struggled to recognize the continuity between various segments of their history, resulting in a compromised identity. The transition from Peter to Paul represents a major transition in Christian origins which created much confusion inside the church community. Who was this renegade Paul and does he represent a split with Petrine Christianity? Was Paul truly an apostle and if so how does he relate to his predecessors? Why does Paul concentrate more effort than the Twelve in reaching the Gentiles? The church in Luke's day struggled with these types of questions, and Luke attempts to demonstrate the continuity between the more Jerusalem-centered ministry of Peter (and the Twelve) and the more expansive ministry of Paul that follows. In order to accomplish this continuity, Luke again utilizes the ancient practice of rhetorical transitions to gradually blend past memories together throughout Acts 8–15.

Paul Remembered in Tradition

Paul was certainly a controversial figure during his lifetime as well as after his death.[1] This section will focus on how Paul was remembered throughout the first century and beyond. Recent scholarship regarding the early reception of Paul will provide a solid background for understanding the various ways Paul was remembered in the ancient world. This will naturally

---

1. While a few scholars might suggest Paul's death as the impetus for Luke's two volumes (based on the ending in Acts 28), Witherington has rightly noted that Acts is not a biography of Paul's life, but rather its intent is "the progress of the gospel and salvation history" (Witherington, *Acts*, 61). For a convincing post-70 dating for Acts, see Bruce, *The Acts*, 12–18.

lead into the next section which will explore how Paul was remembered by Luke in his two-volume historical project.

Since the time of the Tübingen school, the connection between the Paul described in Acts and the image of Paul from the Pauline epistles has been scrutinized. These debates have given rise to two primary ways of handling these texts: either the two images of Paul are irreconcilable, or they are blended into some form of harmonization.[2] The classic example of the thesis of incompatibility lies in Philipp Vielhauer's seminal and controversial article in 1951,[3] which forced scholars to respond with a more balanced understanding of the various ways Paul was received during the first and second centuries.[4] Major studies in the past two decades have focused on how Paul was reconfigured in the first and second centuries in order to keep his significance alive for their audiences. These more recent studies have utilized primarily two methods that have significantly reshaped the landscape of Pauline reception history: rhetoric and narratology.[5] Recently, rhetorical studies on the NT have multiplied, focusing both on the discursive arguments of the Pauline letters and on the narrative-rhetorical techniques used in the Lukan corpus. With the Tübingen School and its trademark *Tendenzkritik*, it was Luke alone as a theologian who reshaped tradition in order to defend or promote the integrity of the uniting church. Recent rhetorical studies, however, have demonstrated that Paul also rhetorically shaped his epistles based on his specific ecclesiastical situations. Scholarship no longer holds to the thoughts of F. C. Baur that the undisputed Pauline letters are the norm against which all later tendentious literature must be evaluated.

The second method that has shifted the paradigm concerning the reception of Paul in the early church is "narratology." Much recent scholarship has examined the potential of narratives to convey complex ideas. Many have begun to realize that the narrative configuration of Paul's life is not inferior to the pure discourse of the Pauline letters.

Daniel Marguerat has recently proposed a new paradigm for understanding the early reception of Paul. He rightly notes that it is anachronistic

---

2. Marguerat covers the primary divergences between the given facts of Acts and of the letters. Marguerat, "Paul," 71.

3. Vielhauer, "On the 'Paulinism,'" 33–50. For a slightly more balanced view, see Roloff, "Die Paulus-Darstellung des Lukas," 510–31.

4. See Porter, *The Paul of Acts*, 187–206.

5. Moessner, "Mediator," 319.

to imagine Luke writing a history of Paul with the letters of the apostle in front of him, since these letters were not collected and assembled until the very end of the first century. Rather, Marguerat notes that between the death of Paul (ca. 60) and the year 100, Paul's heritage was preserved by a variety of means.[6] Specifically, he mentions that the reception of Paul is organized around three poles: documentary, biographical, and doctoral. The "documentary" pole refers to how Paul was remembered as a writer, as his writings were collected and assembled. The "biographical" pole refers to how Paul was celebrated as a spokesman of the gospel message and a missionary to the nations. The "doctoral" pole refers to those treating Paul as a doctor of the church, as they expand his ecclesiology and ethics. Marguerat notes that all three poles were simultaneous at the end of the first century and represented various strategies to preserve the memories of the figure Paul and make him relevant for their specific church community.[7]

This movement away from the restrictive theories of incompatibility and harmonization has allowed all the canonical texts concerning Paul to be evaluated in their own right. Regarding the Lukan portrait of Paul, Marguerat states, "It is therefore inadequate to measure the Lukan historiographical reliability by a norm constituted by the corpus of Pauline writings, precisely because these writing in and of themselves did not constitute the norm of Pauline tradition."[8]

Certainly the largest collection of writings that evidence the significance and meaning of the figure Paul are found in the New Testament canon. In the earlier non-disputed Pauline letters, it is clear that Paul was a controversial figure, causing division and heated debate at every stop. He constantly defended the legitimacy of his apostolic authority (Gal 1:1–24; 2 Cor 10). It is also evident that conflict existed between himself and the Christian leadership at Jerusalem (Gal 2:11–14). These earlier letters also exhibit clear signs that other Christian missionaries were in competition with Paul (Phil 1:15–20).

While space does not allow us to enter the complex debates surrounding the authorship of the later disputed Pauline epistles, it should be noted that these documents (whether written by Paul or a Paulinist) demonstrate

---

6. Marguerat rightly notes that the memory of Paul would primarily be preserved through oral tradition preserved in the communities he founded, rather than primarily in the literary epistles he produced. Marguerat, "Paul," 75.

7. Ibid., 74.

8. Ibid., 75.

the great influence of the figure Paul in Asia.[9] In the Epistles of Ephesians and Colossians, Paul describes himself as one with uncontested authority to reveal Christian mysteries to these Asian cities (Eph 3:1–13; Col 1:24—2:5). In the Pastoral Epistles, Paul describes himself as a prototype (ὑποτύπωσιν) for all subsequent believers (1 Tim 1:16), as well as someone who still causes significant division in Asia (2 Tim 1:15).[10] The strong influence of this figure is clear, which naturally led to conflicting opinions of Paul's rightful place in salvation history.

Written contemporaneously with Luke-Acts, *1 Clement* demonstrates that various stories were circulating surrounding the life and mission of Paul. *First Clement* 5.5–7 details some aspects of Paul's persecution and death, and observes that "he reached the farthest limits of the west" (ἐπὶ τὸ τέρμα τῆς δύσεως ἐλθών), likely indicating the evangelization of Spain. It is also notable that later in *1 Clement*, the author speaks of 1 Cor 1:11–15, describing how the early church became divided between the major leaders such as Paul, Cephas, and Apollos. Clement of Rome appeals to 1 Corinthians to squelch the division in his own day.

Likewise, 2 Peter 3:15–16 demonstrates that the letters of Paul presented some difficulty, which led to misinterpretations and quarrels among the church community addressed there. The author states, καὶ ὁ ἀγαπητὸς ἡμῶν ἀδελφὸς Παῦλος κατὰ τὴν δοθεῖσαν αὐτῷ σοφίαν ἔγραψεν ὑμῖν, ὡς καὶ ἐν πάσαις ταῖς ἐπιστολαῖς λαλῶν ἐν αὐταῖς περὶ τούτων ἐν αἷς ἐστιν δυσνόητά τινα ἃ οἱ ἀμαθεῖς καὶ ἀστήρικτοι στρεβλώσουσιν ὡς καὶ τὰς λοιπὰς γραφὰς πρὸς τὴν ἰδίαν αὐτῶν ἀπώλειαν. Clearly, Paul's teachings from his epistles were interpreted in various ways at the end of the first century.

Acts of Paul represents a later stage of the reception of Paul. In this biographical work in the mid-second century,[11] Paul is venerated to the level of a saint. The author depicts a Pauline figure who mirrors the figure of Christ. At one point, Thecla looks around for Paul and sees "the Lord sitting in the form of Paul," and when she fixes her eyes on him, he departs to heaven

---

9. Witherington makes a solid case for the Pauline authorship of Ephesians and Colossians. Witherington, *The Letters*, 1–36. He also make the case for the Pauline authorship of the Pastoral Epistles. Witherington, *Letters and Homilies*, 23–75. However, see Wolter, "The Development," 50–69. See also Sterling, "From the 'Least of All the Saints,'" 220–44.

10. Wolter, *Die Pastoralbriefe*, 27–64.

11. Tertullian attributes this work to an elder who was an admirer of Paul but not highly inspired (*De Baptismo* 17.5).

(3.21).¹² Likewise, Christ takes the appearance of Paul to reassure Thecla before the ordeal. Also, as Paul is in prison, Christ comes to the rescue: "a young man resembling the body of Paul, lighting not with a lantern, but with the radiance of his body, preceded them until they reached the sea" (9.20). Even after his decapitation by Nero, Paul comes back to life in resurrection appearance similar to those of Jesus in the Gospels (14.6).

What we have observed in the various strands of Pauline reception at the end of the first century and into the second century is a tendency to elevate Paul's status and even defend this historical figure. The earlier authentic Pauline epistles make clear that Paul's authority was highly contested, and following Paul's death, the church took it upon themselves to reconcile the contested issues surrounding Paul's life and ministry. Different authors have gone about this in different ways depending on genre and other exigencies, but there seems to be a general movement to herald the figure Paul as a significant missionary with an indispensable message for the contemporary audience. However, rather than idealize the figure Paul, both epistolary and historiographical strands of Pauline reception retain some negative elements of Paul's life. Paul is still described as a prisoner involved in major resistance, but this is developed into an admirable attribute to be imitated. It is clear that this figure caused controversy not only in his lifetime, but well beyond into the second century. Luke's audience would certainly have felt the tension surrounding this individual and would have likely had many questions surrounding the place of Paul in salvation history.

Lukan Remembrances of Peter and Paul

The relationship between Peter (and the Jerusalem church) and Paul (and the subsequent expansion to the nations) in the book of Acts has been thoroughly examined since the Tübingen School. Coleman Baker has noted how this relationship has gone through three basic methodological phases: a *historical* quest, a *literary* quest, and a *new identity-forming* quest.¹³ During the earliest phase, the historical quest, epitomized by the Tübingen School, scholars worked on a historical reconstruction behind the text of Acts in which Peter and Paul were a part of two opposing Christian factions. This phase was followed by a literary quest in which Lukan scholars began to

12. Schneemelcher and Wilson, *New Testament Apocrypha*.
13. Baker, *Identity*, xvi.

examine the text itself instead of the history behind the text. According to Baker, this naturally led into the most recent phase of an identity-forming quest, in which scholars have searched for how the text of Acts affected its first audiences (and also modern audiences).[14]

The current chapter is concerned primarily with the third phase, exploring how Luke has rhetorically arranged his narrative to reshape the memories of his late first-century audience. However, it would be an error to simply ignore the historical backdrop behind Luke-Acts as some recent narrative studies have done. In what follows, I will examine the rhetorical force of Luke's arrangement in light of his current historical situation. As has been demonstrated above, much controversy surrounding the relationship between Peter (and the Twelve) and Paul continued into the second century,[15] and it was the goal of Luke to demonstrate that the ministries of these two individuals were not incompatible. However, even beyond these two individuals, Luke is concerned to clarify the larger transitional shift in early Christianity. Not only was there conflict surrounding Peter and Paul, but also conflict existed surrounding the full inclusion of non-Judean Christians into the Christ group. Michele Murray notes that "boundaries between nascent Christianity and Judaism remained fluid well beyond the period of Paul who is sometimes incorrectly perceived as having successfully established a distinct identity exclusive of Judaism."[16] Murray also notes how some of the letters of Ignatius demonstrate that this tension existed well into the second century.[17] As Baker states, "The presence of diverse perspectives on Paul (and Peter?) and the inclusion (and exclusion) of non-Judeans into the Christ movement in Luke's authorial audience helps shed light on Luke's presentation of Peter and Paul and the anticipated response on the part of the audience."[18] In fact, the arrangement of the Acts narrative highlights the continuity of salvation history at this juncture.

In his work, *The Book of Acts*, Martin Dibelius states, "Although the division [of Acts] into two parts is so clear, it is difficult to find exactly where

---

14. For a similar assessment of the trajectory of Lukan studies in general, see Spencer, "Acts," 381.

15. For information on Paul's many opponents, see the following: Lightfoot, *Galatians*; Lüdemann, *Opposition*; Schmithals, *Paul*; Sumney *Identifying*.

16. Murray, *Playing*, 83–91, 124.

17. See especially *Magn* 8.1–2, 9.1–2; 10.3; *Phil.* 4.1; 6.1. She also notes the book of Revelation evidences "that Christian Judaizing was a persistent phenomenon in Asia Minor in the late first and early second century CE" (Murray, *Playing*, 82). See Rev 3:9.

18. Baker, *Identity*, 65.

the author himself envisaged the break."[19] This is an accurate assessment, and Lukan scholars have struggled to identify the demarcation between the first and second halves of the Book of Acts. The problem is that commentators have used modern literary conventions to attempt to artificially divide the book in half. Most see some type of literary break at 13:1 (and rightly so),[20] but rarely do scholars pay adequate attention to the rhetorical transition leading up to this break. There is certainly a shift in the character focus from Peter to Paul at this juncture, but scholars have not spent enough time dwelling on the extreme efforts on the part of Luke to show continuity between these two individuals (and the larger movements they represent).[21]

Luke weaves the Petrine and Pauline narratives together through foreshadowing and retrospective elements in this chain-link transition. The larger Petrine narrative block (Acts 1:1—12:25) is briefly interrupted to anticipate Paul's expansion in the following chapters (13:1ff). The following rhetorical structure is thus created:

A	Peter's Ministry in Jerusalem	Acts 1:1—12:25
b	Foreshadowing Paul's Expansion to the Nations	Acts 9:1–31; 11:19–30; 12:25
a	Retrospective Look at Peter	Acts 12:1–24
B	Paul's Expansion to the Nations	Acts 13:1—28:31

So Luke has developed an A-b-a/B structure to weave these two major narrative blocks together. In fact, in order to further tighten these sections together, Saul is introduced even earlier in a brief appearance at 7:58—8:1, while Peter is briefly reintroduced at 15:7–11. Concerning the alternating of Petrine and Pauline narrative blocks, Johnson states, "By this subtle alternation, [Luke] has accomplished two important narrative impressions: first, the reader inevitably sees the career of Saul (Paul) as intimately involved and entwined with that of the other missionaries; second, the reader sees the unprecedented and dangerous initiative toward the Gentiles being taken first, not by the suspect former persecutor, but by Peter (Acts

---

19. Dibelius, *The Book of Acts*, 4. Here Dibelius also notes that in ancient times they called this the "Acts of the Apostles" even though after chapter 6 you really don't hear all that much about the "Apostles" who were with Jesus.

20. See Fitzmyer, *The Acts*, 494. Also, Charles Talbert differentiates Acts 1–12 and 13–28 through seven literary parallels occurring throughout both sections of the text. Talbert, *Literary Patterns*, 23–26.

21. F. C. Baur highlights the importance of Paul to early Christianity in *Paul: The Apostle*, 1:3–4. For a more recent and nuanced assessment, see Dunn, *Beginning from Jerusalem*, 539–41.

10–11)."[22] Luke is obviously concerned to show the continuity between these two phases of recent history and throughout the rest of this chapter it will be observed how he utilized rhetorical transitions to achieve this mnemonic arranging of the past.

Peter's Ministry in Jerusalem (Acts 1:1—12:25)

The first half of Acts highlights the work of Peter, the primary spokesman for the Twelve Apostles.[23] While Luke focuses on the main character of Peter, it becomes clear that this individual represents the core leadership team in Jerusalem. Baker has demonstrated how Luke uses the main characters of Peter and Paul as prototypes of Judean and non-Judean Christ followers in the early church. He states, "The narrative of Acts attempts the recategorization of Judean and non-Judean Christ followers and those on either side of the debate over non-Judean inclusion in the Christ movement into a common ingroup by presenting Peter and Paul as prototypical of a common superordinate Christian identity in the midst of diversity and conflict within the Christ movement in the last decade of the first century CE."[24]

From early on in Acts, Luke places Peter on center stage as the primary spokesman for the Eleven and a representative of the more Jerusalem-centered Christianity. As the narrative moves closer to Paul, Luke focuses much attention on the transition leading up to this shift in early Christianity. Acts 8–12 marks a significant turning point for this early movement, as Luke describes the gradual transition leading up to a prominent Gentile mission headed by Paul. It is important that Luke demonstrates that this transition is orchestrated by God, and more specifically by the Holy Spirit, rather than only human agents. Of the 70 references to the Holy Spirit in Acts, seventeen are found in Acts 8–12, demonstrating the importance of divine guidance during this transition section. Throughout Acts 8–12, the Holy Spirit is the facilitating agent through whom the church is able to multiply, and Luke takes care to narrate the Spirit's involvement at each stage in this expansion of the early church.

---

22. Johnson, *Acts*, 179.

23. The first half of Acts, however, does not exclusively focus on the work of the Twelve or Peter, but also recounts the work of the expanded group of disciples, including Stephen (6:8—7:60), Philip (8:4-40), and even James, the brother of Jesus, as the narrative proceeds.

24. Baker, *Identity*, 1.

As Philip encounters Samaritans for the first time in this narrative, Peter and John are called to make sure the Holy Spirit is present (8:14–17). As Jews and Samaritans are beginning to join forces, it would be crucial for both to experience the Spirit-identity of cultural inclusivity (cf. Luke 9:52–55 for the normal relationship patterns between these two distinct groups in antiquity). By understanding the importance of the Holy Spirit in the bridging of diverse cultures, it becomes clear why Peter and John became infuriated with Simon the magician, when he wishes to turn the Holy Spirit into a source of financial income (8:18–23). As Philip continues to break new missiological ground, the Holy Spirit directs him toward an Ethiopian eunuch along the road from Jerusalem to Gaza (8:26). The Spirit sets up this divine appointment and then miraculously transports Philip to Azotus (8:40). In this literary move, Luke implies the importance of the Holy Spirit in the initial spread of the Word into Africa.

As the narrative shifts from Philip to Saul, the audience is told that Saul is receiving the Holy Spirit during his conversion process in Damascus (9:17). This would be necessary if he is to stop hindering the Word and begin to spread it. The narrative then describes explicitly that the church is multiplying due to the fear of the Lord and *the encouragement of the Holy Spirit* (9:31). The next major moment in early Christian expansion occurs in Acts 10:1ff, as Peter is directed by the Spirit to approach Gentiles with the Word (10:19; 11:12). Peter travels to the house of Cornelius in Caesarea, where he proclaims the Word and the Holy Spirit falls on all who hear the message (10:44; 11:15). The circumcised Jewish believers are said to be astonished that the Holy Spirit is able to be poured on Gentiles (10:45), but Peter states that their claim to the Holy Spirit is as strong as Jews (10:47). As the narrative moves on to describe the spread of the Word beyond Palestine, the Holy Spirit also plays a large role. When the Word spreads to Syrian Antioch, the Jerusalem church sends Barnabas to monitor their activity. Upon seeing the manifestation of the Spirit there, he rejoices since he himself was *full of the Holy Spirit* (11:23–24).

It is also telling that toward the end of the narrative block of Acts 8–12, Luke includes the work of various non-apostles (Stephen, Philip, etc.) in order to ease into Paul's work in 13:1ff. Witherington notes that one of Luke's purposes is to demonstrate how people like Theophilus had come to be involved in a religious phenomenon which originated as a Jewish messianic movement.[25] He states that "this meant that some considerable time

---

25. Concerning the debate surrounding Theophilus, Cornelius, and others as οι

had to be taken to show not only the geographical spread of the movement but also its spread across ethnic barriers and social boundaries."[26] Luke is exercising extreme effort to create a seamless transition between God's work amongst Jews in Judea and the Gentile expansion led by Paul in the second half of Acts.

The rapid expansion of Christianity across ethnic and social boundaries required that Luke occasionally pause to provide summary statements about the spread of the Word of God.[27] These periodic summary statements are found at key junctures in the narrative and serve to further link together the various "panels" of the book of Acts. Acts 6:7 describes that the word of God increased and the Jerusalem disciples multiplied. Acts 9:31 states that the church throughout Galilee and Judea was built up and multiplied by the Holy Spirit. Acts 12:24 notes that the Word of God grew and multiplied and also involved Paul and Barnabas. Acts 16:5 shows the churches strengthened in faith and increasing in number as Paul and Timothy are heading through Asia Minor. Acts 19:20 notes that the word of God prevailed as all the residents of Asia hear. These summary statements are yet another technique utilized by Luke to create mnemonic cohesion in his historiography.

In addition to these summary *statements*, Luke also included the well-known summary *passages* to link together various episodes of the early chapters of Acts (2:42–47; 4:32–37; 5:12–16; 8:1b–4).[28] These summary passages are found only in the first eight chapters of Acts, and offer further evidence that Luke is developing a legato narrative from the very beginning of the book of Acts. Some scholars have noted that this is due to the fact that Luke had fewer and less extensive sources for his narratives dealing with the early church in Jerusalem.[29] Regardless of Luke's available sources concerning Acts 1–8, what is clear is that he goes to great lengths to bind these episodes together in order to help facilitate his vision of a continuous salvation history. Luke connects these seemingly detached events in a way that provided memory reinforcement for his listening audience(s).

φοβουμενοι, see the following: Witherington, *Acts*, 341–44; Barrett, *Acts*, 1:500–501; Lake, "Proselytes," 74–96; Wilcox, "The God-Fearers," 102–22.

26. Witherington, *Acts*, 339.

27. Ibid., 74.

28. Witherington helpfully distinguishes between summary *statements* and summary *passages*. Ibid., 157–60.

29. Ibid., 159.

One significant moment for Luke in the early expansion of Christianity was the Cornelius event. It is extremely telling that Luke marks Peter as the one first responsible for the expansion of Christianity beyond the borders of Judea.[30] Keener notes that historically it is possible that Hellenists evangelized Gentiles before Peter (as indicated by 11:19–21), but for Luke apostolic ratification was necessary to validate full Gentile inclusion in God's covenant people. Keener notes, "For Luke, it was apostolic ratification that proved decisive, confirming the continuity between Jerusalem (and the church's Jewish heritage stressed in the Gospel) and the Gentile mission (stressed in Acts). The conversion of Cornelius is thus a major turning point in the work's plot development."[31] It is also significant that Luke deems the Cornelius event so important in nascent Christianity that he repeats it three times in the next several chapters, the last summary of the events occurring in Acts 15, which further weaves the characters of Peter and Paul together. The events set in motion by Peter's interactions with Cornelius develop a crisis of sorts that is partially resolved as the Jerusalem Council endorses an outright mission to the Gentiles in Acts 15. While Luke describes the Cornelius event as a major turning point in the narrative, he clearly states that the impetus to move in a Gentile direction comes directly from God. This is seen through the various visions and messengers from God who direct Christianity in a certain direction.

Richard Pervo notes that criteria of importance in the Lukan corpus include length, repetition, and the dense supernatural apparatus of vision and epiphany.[32] This story of the first Gentile conversion in Acts contains all these features and therefore should be viewed as a highly significant segment in the narrative of the early church. Also adding to the significance of this event are the importance of both key characters: Peter, as the leader of the church, and Cornelius, a prominent soldier and citizen.[33] Pervo wisely observes that the primarily Gentile audience of this document already know that the Gentile mission will occur in the midst of difficulties, and so for them the literary pleasure of Acts is learning how this project came about.[34]

---

30. Keener, *Acts*, 1727.
31. Ibid., 1728.
32. Pervo, *Acts*, 264–67.
33. Ibid., 264.
34. Ibid., 265.

The Transition from Peter to Paul

The main point of the Cornelius narrative is clear: God does not show favoritism (10:34). The message is for Jews and Gentiles alike. Luke makes this clear both through the literary structure of his narrative as well as in the explicit statements of Peter. As the segment begins, Luke describes the preparation for a divine appointment between Peter and Cornelius. What is significant here is that Luke creates a parallelism between these two characters that allows the audience to understand that God truly does interact equally with both Jews and Gentiles (10:1-23). The similarities between these two accounts are numerous. Both men have a vision (ὀράματι) while praying to YHWH at a specific Jewish hour of prayer. Both are somewhat confused by the vision, but desire to know the meaning of all this (10:4-6, 13-20). Both refer to God's messenger using the vocative for Lord (κύριε). Both receive commands and obey (10:7-8, 20-23).

If Luke's narrative does not show clearly enough that God interacts equally with both Jews and Gentiles, Peter's discourse makes this explicit at several points (10:34-43; 11:4-17). Peter begins his speech to Cornelius' home with his central point: ἐπ' ἀληθείας καταλαμβάνομαι ὅτι οὐκ ἔστιν προσωπολήμπτης ὁ θεός, ἀλλ' ἐν παντὶ ἔθνει ὁ φοβούμενος αὐτὸν καὶ ἐργαζόμενος δικαιοσύνην δεκτὸς αὐτῷ ἐστιν (10:34-35). In this statement, Peter makes clear that God offers every people group (παντὶ ἔθνει) the opportunity to follow him. This is the first use of the word "all," a word that becomes significant in Peter's rhetoric in this speech. He moves on to state that Jesus is "Lord of *all*" (10:36), that Jesus healed *all* people oppressed by the devil (10:38), the prophets stated that *all* who believe in him will receive forgiveness of sins (10:43). After Peter's message ends, Luke makes this speech a reality by narrating the event that the Holy Spirit fell on *all* who heard the message. There is obviously a message of inclusivity here in this segment.

While this watershed moment in the church's history is filled with the miraculous outpouring of God's promised Holy Spirit, this event is met by some internal resistance from circumcised members of the Jerusalem church. However, after Peter's message, these men evidently understand the truth of God's impartiality. They not only are silenced by Peter's words, but they praise God that He has given Gentiles repentance leading to life (11:18).

Through an examination of the Cornelius events (and the larger context of Acts 8-12), it becomes clear how integral this segment is to the overall rhetorical agenda of Luke. It connects both the material before this and the narrative to come. As for the prior material in Acts, this segment points back to Pentecost, drawing a comparison between these two events. This event at Caesarea Maritima represents an outpouring of the Holy Spirit on the Gentile ethnicity, just as He had been poured out on Jews in Acts 2. Likewise this segment of text becomes somewhat of a culmination/climax of Acts 8–9. Beginning in Acts 8, the Holy Spirit is directing the mission toward foreign ethnicities, starting with the neighboring Samaritans (Acts 8). This is followed by Saul's miraculous conversion and his assigned mission to the Gentiles (Acts 9). On the heels of these events, God arranges the meeting of the Jerusalem church (represented by Peter) with the Gentile nations (Acts 10). This will drive the church outward toward Antioch and beyond (Acts 11:19—12:25). This ethnic expansion will cause internal difficulties, which are somewhat resolved in Acts 15. Then Paul will take up the baton from Peter and carry the message around the Mediterranean world and into the heart of the Roman Empire (Acts 13–28).

Foreshadowing Paul's Expansion to the Nations (Acts 9:1–31; 11:19–30; 12:25)

Luke is careful to share plenty of information about Paul prior to the time he becomes the central character in the narrative (13:1ff). In accordance with ancient rhetorical conventions, Luke has utilized a chain-link transition by first foreshadowing the work of Paul during the first half of Acts which is primarily concerned with Peter and the Jerusalem church. By offering historical information about Paul at this early stage in the narrative, Luke allows his audience time to connect the past memories of Peter with those of Paul. Likewise, this gradual transition allows his audience to place the mission to the Jews adjacent to the Gentile mission in their memories of early Christianity. Luke is rhetorically structuring recent history for his struggling church audience.

The earliest reference to Paul (or Saul) is the mention of his role in the stoning of Stephen and his persecution of the Christian church in Jerusalem (7:59—8:3). In his shaping of recent history, Luke is confined by the tradition shared by himself and his audience. Both are aware of Paul's tainted past, and Luke does not simply expunge these events from the record books.[35] It was actually important to address this event (albeit ever so briefly), in order to reconcile them with the prominent place Paul took in

---

35. Clivaz, "Rumour," 264–81.

The Transition from Peter to Paul

the early church. The church at the end of the first century surely struggled to understand the transformation of Paul, and it is Luke who undertook the challenge in his narration of his conversion. As Johnson states, "How can the narrator make plausible one of history's most stunning and inexplicable turnabouts, when Paul himself, who based his authority as an apostle precisely on this experience (1 Cor 9:1; 15:8) was always required to include as part of his apologetic the embarrassing fact that he had been a 'persecutor of the Church' (1 Cor 15:8; Gal 1:11–17; Phil 3:6; 1 Tim 1:13), without ever finding universal acceptance of his claims or credentials?"[36] In order to accomplish this delicate rhetorical task, Luke actually provides three versions of Paul's conversion (9:1–19; 22:3–21; 26:9–18). Johnson states, "The turning of a Pharisaic persecutor into the apostle of the Gentiles is a paradox so profound that it requires multiple retellings, with each version bringing out some further nuance of significance."[37] The fact that the first conversion account is found in the first half of Acts serves to further link the work of Paul with the work of Peter and the Jerusalem leadership.

Luke follows up Paul's conversion by a brief look at Paul's initial ministry in and around Damascus (9:20–31).[38] Scholars have spent much effort comparing Luke's account of Paul here with Paul's autobiographical information on corresponding events in Gal 1:15–23. The divergences between the two accounts, however, is the result of specific rhetorical motives by each author and scholars would do well to grant each their sincerity and recognize that each had their own interests in shaping the narrative as they did. In his letter to the Galatians, Paul is attempting to establish his independence from Jerusalem in order to defend the authenticity of his apostleship. On the contrary, Luke attempts to highlight the connection between Paul and the Jerusalem church in order to develop an overall cohesiveness between their work. Johnson states, "Luke's interest is showing how the gospel moved out into the Gentile world in continuity with the restored people of God in Jerusalem. Luke therefore establishes narrative links between Paul and the other apostles."[39]

---

36. Johnson, *The Acts*, 166.

37. Ibid.

38. Witherington notes the similarities between the initial messages of Jesus (Luke 4:1-30) and Paul (Acts 9:20-30). Witherington, *Acts*, 320. Luke records these similarities to further weave the story of Paul into the stories of his predecessors.

39. Johnson, *Acts*, 173–74.

After a few chapters dedicated to Peter and the pouring out of the Holy Spirit to Gentiles (Acts 10:1—11:18), Luke again reminds the audience of the figure of Paul. Acts 11:19 reminds the audience of the questionable past of Paul by directly speaking of the scattering of God's people following the stoning of Stephen. The text of 11:19 matches verbatim with that of 8:4, Οἱ μὲν οὖν διασπαρέντες, as Luke reconnects the story of Paul with the preceding narrative. At this point, however, Luke records a Paul who facilitates the expansion of Christianity beyond Jerusalem borders compared to the Saul who previously attempted to thwart the spread of this new movement. Barnabas and Paul are described as cultivating the growing church in Syrian Antioch (11:26),[40] and even begin raising support for the believers struggling through the famine in Jerusalem. It is notable how Luke utilizes Barnabas as a further link between the Jerusalem church and Paul. Acts 4:36–37 demonstrated how Barnabas was submissive to the apostles' leadership, receiving a new name from them and laying his possessions at their feet. Luke describes this "son of consolation" as a mediator between Saul and the church (9:27; 11:22).[41]

Retrospective Look at Peter (Acts 12:1–24)

The placement of the prison narrative in Acts 12 continues to stir up controversy among Lukan scholars.[42] After describing the expansion of Christianity as far as Phoenecia, Cyprus and Syrian Antioch (11:19) and introducing the ministry of Paul (and Barnabas) at Antioch (11:25–30), Luke redirects the narrative to Jerusalem to describe Peter's imprisonment and escape (12:1–19) as well as the death of Herod (12:20–23). Longenecker has rightly noted that this seemingly "out of place" narrative has been purposefully arranged in order to create a chain-link rhetorical transition between Peter and Paul.[43] While describing important historical information regarding Peter and Herod, this section of the narrative allows the

---

40. For an extensive look at the historical metropolis of Antioch, see Keener, *Acts*, 1833–40.

41. The Western version of Acts 11:25 states that Barnabas had to "exhort" Paul to come with him to Antioch, highlighting the "controversial" nature of Paul. Witherington, *Acts*, 370.

42. For a list of various exegetical solutions, see Longenecker, *Rhetoric*, 176–92.

43. Ibid.

The Transition from Peter to Paul

audience to "pause" and synthesize the somewhat unorthodox movements of the early church thus far.

This "pause" not only allows one to think ahead toward the future mission to the Gentiles, but also allows the audience an opportunity to reflect on the earlier work done in and around Jerusalem. Witherington notes that "this story serves to help justify the shift in focus in the narrative from Jerusalem to Antioch and then even farther west. Jerusalem was not going to be the kind of place which, in the future, missionaries to the Gentiles, whether Peter or Paul or others, could call home base for long."[44]

It is significant how Luke describes Peter's departure from Jerusalem. It is not simply an escape, nor does Luke describe it as a defeat for the church. Rather, Luke is careful to note that Ὁ δὲ λόγος τοῦ θεοῦ ηὔξανεν καὶ ἐπληθύνετο (12:24). Luke takes this opportunity to describe how Herod's persecution of the Jerusalem church has brought an end to the first phase of missionary expansion of the church, which originated and was organized by Jewish Christian missionaries from Jerusalem.[45] While Luke describes that Peter left Jerusalem for ἕτερον τόπον (12:17), he is purposefully vague since the narrative is shifting away from Peter's story toward Paul's.

Paul's Expansion to the Nations (Acts 13:1—28:31)

While there have been clear Gentile conversions prior to Acts 13, the missions have not been planned by the church. Here at 13:1ff., we see the inaugural efforts by the church at planned evangelism of the Gentiles. Also, at this point the main focus of the narrative shifts almost exclusively to the figure Paul, marking 13:1 as a new rhetorical unit in the Lukan narrative.

If one recalls Luke's stated aims in Luke 1:1–4 to provide ἀσφάλεια to a mixed audience regarding the connectedness of various phases of early Christianity, then it should come as no surprise that we do not find a renegade Paul in the second half of Acts who abandons Israel to deliver a suspect message to only Gentiles. It has already been demonstrated how Luke has architecturally structured the early part of Acts to include brief foreshadows of Paul and the expanded ministry to the ends of the earth. Here in the second half of Acts, Johnson states that we find "an apostle whose divine commission is confirmed by prophetic election and the charge of the Church, whose activities are not only filled with the prophetic spirit but

---

44. Witherington, *Acts*, 383.
45. Schnabel, *Acts*, 528.

also mirror those of Jesus and Peter before him, who remains in constant contact with Jerusalem, and who until the very end of the story tries to convert his fellow Jews."[46]

Luke validates Paul in two ways through this initial passage in Acts 13:1–3.[47] First, the passage indicates that Paul (and Barnabas) are thoroughly enmeshed in the Antiochean church. Paul and Barnabas are listed among the leaders of the church community, where they have served for a whole year (11:26) exercising their gifts as prophets and teachers, while fasting and praying with the church there. It appears that Luke even emphasizes the amount of time that Paul and Barnabas were in Antioch with the phrase ἐνιαυτὸν ὅλον. Second, the Holy Spirit himself intervenes directly to set apart Paul and Barnabas for their missionary travels, as Luke records twice in case the audience missed the first reference (13:2, 4). There is certainly divine guidance in this transitional phase of nascent Christianity.

The narrative structure over the next couple chapters allows Luke to introduce the missionary travels of Paul, while the Jerusalem Council in Acts 15 will officially legitimize his ministry and further tie it to the ministry of the Apostles in the first half of Acts. It is at the Jerusalem Council that the human church finally catches up to the divine initiative and decrees itself a proponent of a mission to save all of humanity. This Council also provides Luke an opportunity to demonstrate the continuity between the various phases in early Christianity. Johnson states, "The discussion [at the Jerusalem Council] provides the opportunity to emphasize the essential *continuity* between these stages in the divine plan: the inclusion of the Gentiles does not mean the replacement of 'Israel' but its expansion; the elimination of Mosaic *ethos* (custom) for the Gentiles does not mean the elimination of Torah, but rather the fulfillment of its prophetic intention, 'made known from long ago' (15:18), as well as the continuation of those aspects of Torah that have always applied to the proselyte and sojourner."[48] As Paul's missionary journeys geographically reach further away from Israel, he never loses sight of the Jewish heritage of the church.

Luke utilizes the material in Acts 15 to highlight that Paul was not the first to advocate the inclusion of non-Judeans into the people of God. Paul is no renegade, but rather continuing in the trajectory that God has been moving throughout recent history. When debate arose concerning

---

46. Johnson, *Acts*, 225.
47. Ibid.
48. Ibid., 268.

the inclusion of uncircumcised individuals, it is Peter who offers the first words of defense at the Jerusalem Council. He states, "My brothers, you know that in the early days (ἡμερῶν ἀρχαίων) God made a choice among you, that I should be the one through whom the Gentiles would hear the message of the good news and become believers" (Acts 15:7). Next, it is James who offers his defense: "My brothers, listen to me. Simeon has related how God first looked favorably on the Gentiles (ἐθνῶν), to take from among them a people (λαὸν) for his name" (Acts 15:13–14). Parsons notes that James replaces the normal word for non-Judeans (εθνός) with the usual word for the people of God (λαός), demonstrating that God's people has expanded to include non-Judeans.[49] James proceeds to further ground his decision in the words of the prophets, who record that God has been making these things known from long ago (ἀπ' αἰῶνος) (Acts 15:15–18). Then, and only then, is Paul appointed by the Jerusalem church to spread this decision to non-Judeans. Luke utilizes the Jerusalem Council to bind Paul to the Jerusalem church, presenting him as a bridge figure to connect what God has done in the past with what he wants to do in the future.[50] Paul's resulting missionary journeys throughout the rest of the narrative are therefore grounded in the foundation laid by Peter and the Jerusalem church which he represents.

Conclusion

Much controversy surrounded the figure Paul in the first century, resulting in a variety of diverse commemorations of this individual. Both canonical witnesses and extrabiblical sources demonstrate the significant influence of this individual throughout the Mediterranean basin. During the latter part of the first century and into the second century, communities were divided concerning this unique missionary. It has been suggested in this chapter that this resulted in the development of staccato narratives that led to mental gaps between the early Jerusalem church and Paul. It has further been suggested that Luke established a legato narrative in order to intricately weave the characters of Peter and Paul together, and in the process

---

49. Parsons, *Acts*, 212.

50. Baker suggests that this Council has resulted in a new superordinate identity that does not abolish ancient ethnic customs, but rather allows for subgroups to be recategorized under the umbrella category of "Christ followers" (Baker, *Identity*, 155).

join the predominantly Jewish Christianity represented in Acts 1–8 with the outright Gentile missions of Paul in Acts 13–28.

Peter and Paul stand as highly significant mnemonic artifacts for the early church, and Luke has chosen to commemorate these two figures in a uniquely elaborate arrangement. Unlike other traditions surrounding these two figures, Luke has gone to extreme lengths to highlight the connectedness of the ministries of Peter and Paul. His efforts to bind these two figures through rhetorical transitions results in an intricate arrangement that influences the sequence of events in Acts.

Early on in the book of Acts, Peter emerges as the primary spokesman for early Christianity. In Acts 10–11, Luke even describes Peter as the primary human agent in establishing the inclusion of non-Judeans into the people of God. However, while the first half of Acts is concerned primarily with Peter and the Jerusalem church, Luke begins to introduce the character Paul in order to create a continuous transition in the minds of his audience. This transitional overlap in Acts 8–12 presents time for the audience to pause and reconfigure their somewhat staccato memories into a more continuous remembrance of the past. To further bind the characters of Peter and Paul, Luke reintroduces Peter in Acts 12 and again at Acts 15 as a reminder that Paul's actions in the interim are not self-governed. Rather, it is God who orchestrates every major movement in the history of the early church and Peter and Paul are in alignment with this divine plan.

Conclusion

IN THE INTRODUCTION TO this book, I stated my central proposal that Luke structures his rhetorical transitions in order to facilitate his vision of salvation history as a continuous work in progress, and in the process reminds the late first-century church that there were not irreconcilable differences between the various developmental stages of early Christianity. In the chapters that followed, I explained that the best way to describe Luke's two-volume project is legato historiography. Luke desired to present a fresh narrative of past events in place of the staccato memories of the late first-century church. In this process, he reassured his audience(s) that the seeming gaps in nascent Christianity were not, in fact, irreconcilable. Rather, Luke's narrative arrangement highlights the continuity between the various phases of early Christianity, and God is presented as the orchestrator of those events.

The first two chapters provided the necessary methodological and historical background for the exegetical work that would follow. In chapter 1, my socio-rhetorical methodology was described in detail to set the stage for a fresh reading of Luke-Acts. I began with an examination of how memory functions, specifically noting the structure of remembrances when people shape recollections of the past. Utilizing social memory theory, I then highlighted that ancient historians in Luke's milieu highly valued structuring history into legato narratives. It was further demonstrated that Luke himself shaped a legato narrative of recent Christianity, primarily through the use of rhetorical transitions. It was therefore concluded that these combined lenses of memory and rhetoric best highlight Luke's purpose for his two-volume historiography.

In chapter 2, I reviewed the socio-historical background for Luke and his audience(s) in the late first century. It was concluded that Luke-Acts was written by a Gentile with strong Jewish roots and intended for a largely Gentile Christian target audience in urban centers. It was shown

Luke's Legato Historiography

that, in general, urban Christian churches at this time would have felt some confusion surrounding the connectedness of nascent Christianity. Through an examination of Luke's Preface (1:1–4), it was further concluded that Luke felt it necessary to properly arrange (καθεξῆς) his narrative in order for his specific target audience(s) to fully understand the continuity of salvation history.

The second half of this book (chapters 3 through 6) examined the four primary rhetorical transitions used by Luke throughout his two volumes. In each of these four chapters, I have shown how various personages in the early church were treated as historical artifacts and commemorated in a staccato fashion which resulted in some confusion. I then highlighted how Luke commemorated these artifacts in a legato arrangement for the purpose of demonstrating the connectedness of salvation history.

In chapter 3, I observed that confusion surrounded the relationship between JBap and Jesus at the end of the first century. This led Luke to craft an elaborate rhetorical transition to show continuity between these two figures. Not only did this transition connect the memories of JBap and Jesus, but also presented a smooth bridge between the world of the OT and the new kingdom inaugurated by Jesus. In Luke 1–4, the audience(s) had time to synthesize their memories of JBap and Jesus (and the eras they represented), as Luke reassured them of an overall connected salvation history.

In chapter 4, I noticed how misunderstandings surrounded the transfer of leadership from Jesus to his disciples. In response, Luke shaped a lengthy rhetorical transition in Luke 5–18 in order to persuade his audience that God orchestrated the shift in leadership away from the traditional Jewish regime to a wider group of followers including the Twelve, the Seventy-two, and women. This rhetorical move foreshadows the expanded leadership group that Luke's audience encounters in the book of Acts.

In chapter 5, I suggested that the confusion surrounding the epochal shift from Jesus to the Holy Spirit warranted a narrative explanation from Luke. In Luke 24—Acts 2, a sophisticated rhetorical transition gives the audience an opportunity to understand the shift from Jesus' ascension to the outpouring of the Holy Spirit. With this transition, Luke persuades his audience of the connectedness of salvation history at this important juncture and weaves together the two volumes of his historiography in the process.

In chapter 6, I observed that significant questions existed surrounding the individual Paul and how he related to Peter and the church in Jerusalem. In response, Luke has crafted a rhetorical transition in order to highlight the

Conclusion

continuity between the early Christian center at Jerusalem and the later outward movement of Paul toward Gentiles. Throughout this transition, Luke persuades his audience that it is God who has orchestrated the major shifts at this important juncture in the history of the church, and Peter and Paul are both in alignment with this continuous plan of salvation history.

There are several implications that result from this book. First, this study has affirmed the traditional stance on several major aspects of Luke-Acts. Through a comparison of Luke-Acts with other ancient historians, this study has confirmed that the best genre category for these two volumes remains Greek historiography. Likewise, this study has further demonstrated that Luke and Acts were written by the same author with the intention of being delivered as a unified narrative.

Second, this study has shown that individual passages in Luke-Acts should always be examined in light of the overall rhetorical macro-structure of these two volumes. Exegetical problems will result from isolating certain passages from Luke's larger rhetorical program. For example, studies in Lukan pneumatology will benefit from examining the Day of Pentecost in light of the transition connecting Luke's two volumes. Likewise, individual passages in Luke's Central Section will gain fresh meaning when it is understood as an explanation of the transition between Jesus and his disciples.

Third, this study has methodological implications for the NT. While rhetoric has been a blossoming field for some time now, this study has shown how it can be augmented by modern sociological theories (particularly memory theory). While identifying the rhetorical units of NT passages certainly has value, it also has its limitations. The social sciences can assist in asking new questions of these rhetorical devices. Specifically, this study demonstrated how social memory theory can provide the pulsing organs within the skeleton of ancient rhetoric. In this way, the rhetorical structure is not seen simply as a conventional technique, but actually shapes the theology and offers a vehicle for theological thought.

Fourth, this study has implications for the connectedness of Scripture. At a time when biblical scholarship has become so fragmented and specialized, it is rare to find someone actually attempting to connect portions of Scripture. It would be prudent to follow the example of Luke and go to extreme efforts to connect the strands of salvation history in order to demonstrate God's consistency. The varied theologies of the HB and NT should be held together in tension to provide a fuller portrait of how God has orchestrated a multitude of human agents toward a common goal.

This study has also provided opportunities for future research in several arenas. First, much work still remains to be done in the area of rhetorical transitions in antiquity, in both Greco-Roman literature at large as well as more specifically in the NT. It would be particularly interesting to examine how the other canonical gospels shaped their remembrances of the past at transition points. Perhaps, one could even examine the rhetorical macro-structure of the Western version of the Acts of the Apostles. Also, a full-scale investigation of Paul's use of rhetorical transitions in his letters has yet to be undertaken.

Second, there is further work to be done in the area of sociology. I feel that I have just examined the tip of the iceberg in regard to the social implications of undergoing life-changing transitions. It would be interesting to examine various periods throughout church history to investigate the impact of major transition periods on everyday church life. It would also be helpful to further explore how one's social situation can impact the structure of one's rhetoric. Another area with significant potential is to further pursue the relationship between social memory theory and ancient rhetoric.

Third, this study has brought up several areas for further research within the Lukan corpus itself. Yet to be done is a large-scale investigation of Lukan pneumatology that takes into consideration the larger rhetorical macro-structure of the two volumes. Likewise, my fresh socio-rhetorical methodology could also assist in discovering the organization of the many seemingly random teachings throughout Luke's Central Section.

Fourth, this study has provided avenues for further research regarding historical reconstructions of early Christianity. More detailed research is needed in the book of Acts to properly distinguish between straightforward, linear historical accounts and the rhetorical interweaving of events. A more accurate methodology is needed when utilizing Luke's highly rhetorical narrative to reconstruct historical timelines of events in the early church. It could be further beneficial to see an in-depth comparison between Acts and similar works of ancient Greek historiography in this process. Not only is there work to do in the historical reconstruction of the events narrated in Acts, but also in the historical reconstruction of Christianity in the late first century when Luke-Acts was written. Further research is needed to examine the so-called "parting of the ways" between Judaism and Christianity. What can the rhetorical arrangement of Luke-Acts demonstrate about the continuity (or discontinuity) between nascent Christianity and its Jewish roots? How might these conclusions reverberate across the whole of the NT?

There are certainly more questions that will arise from this study outside of those already mentioned. These suggestions, however, should suffice to indicate that the material in this study has generated fresh questions surrounding the church of Luke's day. It is my hope that this study will inspire related research that will continue to produce a clearer picture of the first-century church.

Bibliography

Aelius Theon. *Progymnasmata*. Translated by Michel Patillon. Paris: Les Belles Lettres, 1997.
Alexander, Loveday. *Acts in its Ancient Literary Context*. New York: T. & T. Clark, 2005.
———. "Ancient Book Production and the Gospels." In *The Gospels for All Christians: Rethinking the Gospel Audiences*, edited by Richard Bauckham, 71-111. Grand Rapids: Eerdmans, 1998.
———. "Memory and Tradition in the Hellenistic Schools." In *Jesus in Memory: Traditions in Oral and Scribal Perspectives*, edited by Werner H. Kelber and Samuel Byrskog, 113-53. Waco: Baylor University Press, 2009.
———. *The Preface to Luke's Gospel: Literary Convention and Social Context in Luke 1:1-4 and Acts 1:1*. Cambridge: Cambridge University Press, 1993.
———. "Which Greco-Roman Prologues Most Closely Parallel the Lukan Prologues?" In *Jesus and the Heritage of Israel: Luke's Narrative Claim upon Israel's Legacy*, edited by David P. Moessner, 9-26. Harrisburg, PA: Trinity, 1999.
Aristotle. *Art of Rhetoric*. Translated by J. H. Freese. Loeb Classical Library. Cambridge, MA: Harvard University Press, 1926.
———. *Poetics*. Translated by S. H. Butcher. New York: Dramabook, 1961.
Assmann, Jan. "Collective Memory and Cultural Identity." *New German Critique* 65 (1995) 125-33.
———. *Cultural Memory and Early Civilization: Writing, Remembrance, and Political Imagination*. Cambridge: Cambridge University Press, 2011.
———. *Das kulturelle Gedachtnis. Schrift, Erinnerung und politische Identitat in fruhen Hochkulturen*. Munich: Beck, 1992.
———. *Religion und kulturelles Gedächtnis: Zehn Studien*. Munich: Beck, 2000.
Aune, David. *The New Testament in Its Literary Environment*. Philadelphia: Westminster, 1987.
———. "The Significance of the Delay of the Parousia for Early Christianity." In *Current Issues in Biblical and Patristic Interpretation*, edited by Gerald F. Hawthorne, 87-109. Grand Rapids: Eerdmans, 1975.
Baer, Hans von. *Der Heilige Geist in den Lukasschriften*. Stuttgart: Kohlhammer, 1926.
Bailey, Kenneth E. "Informal Controlled Oral Tradition and the Synoptic Gospels." *Asia Journal of Theology* 5 (1991) 34-51.
———. "Informal Controlled Oral Tradition and the Synoptic Gospels." *Themelios* 20 (1995) 4-11.

Bibliography

Baker, Coleman. *Identity, Memory, and Narrative in Early Christianity: Peter, Paul, and Recategorization in the Book of Acts*. Eugene, OR: Wipf & Stock, 2011.

Barrett, C. K. *Acts*. International Critical Commentary. 2 vols. New York: T. & T. Clark, 2004.

———. "J. B. Lightfoot as Biblical Commentator." In *Jesus and the Word: And Other Essays*, 15–34. Princeton Theological Monograph Series 41. Eugene, OR: Wipf & Stock, 1995.

———. "Quomodo historia conscribenda sit." *New Testament Studies* 28/3 (1982) 303–20.

———. "The Third Gospel as a Preface to Acts? Some Reflections." In *The Four Gospels 1992. Festschrift Frans Neirynck*, edited by F. Van Segbroeck et al., 1451–66. Leuven: Leuven University Press, 1992.

Bartholomew, Craig, et al., eds. *Reading Luke*. Scripture and Hermeneutics 6. Grand Rapids: Zondervan, 2005.

Bauckham, Richard. *The Gospels for All Christians: Rethinking the Gospel Audiences*. Grand Rapids: Eerdmans, 1998.

———. *Jesus and the Eyewitnesses: The Gospels as Eyewitness Testimony*. Grand Rapids: Eerdmans, 2006.

Baur, F. C. *Kritische Untersuchungen über die kanonischen Evangelien*. 1847.

———. *Paul: The Apostle of Jesus Christ, His Life and Work, His Epistles and Doctrine, A Contribution to a Critical History of Primitive Christianity*. 2 vols. London: Williams and Norgate, 1875–76.

———. *Paulus, der Apostel*. 1845.

———. *Uber den Ursprung*. 1838.

Berger, Peter. *Invitation to Sociology*. Garden City, NY: Doubleday, 1967.

Bird, Michael F. *Jesus and the Origins of the Gentile Mission*. Library of New Testament Studies 331. New York: T. & T. Clark, 2006.

Bock, Darrell. *Luke*. 2 vols. Grand Rapids: Baker, 1994–96.

Bonz, Marianne Palmer. *The Past as Legacy: Luke-Acts and Ancient Epic*. Minneapolis: Fortress, 2000.

Bovon, François. *Luke*. 3 vols. Hermeneia. Minneapolis: Fortress, 2002–13.

———. *Luke the Theologian*. 2nd ed. Waco: Baylor University Press, 2006.

Brown, Raymond E. *The Birth of the Messiah: A Commentary on the Infancy Narratives in the Gospels of Matthew and Luke*. New York: Anchor, 1993.

Bruce, F. F. *The Acts of the Apostles*. Grand Rapids: Eerdmans, 1990.

Büchsel, Friedrich. *Der Geist Gottes im Neuen Testament*. Gütersloh: Bertelsmann, 1926.

Bultmann, Rudolf. *The History of the Synoptic Tradition*. Translated by John Marsh. New York: Harper, 1963.

Burke, Alexander J. *John the Baptist: Prophet and Disciple*. Cincinnati: St. Anthony Messenger, 2006.

Burke, Peter. *History and Social Theory*. 3rd ed. Ithaca, NY: Cornell University Press, 1992.

Burridge, Richard A. "The Gospels and Acts." In *Handbook of Classical Rhetoric in the Hellenistic Period, 330 B.C.–A.D. 400*, edited by S. E. Porter, 507–32. Leiden: Brill, 1997.

———. *What Are the Gospels? A Comparison with Graeco-Roman Biography*. Grand Rapids: Eerdmans, 2004.

Bibliography

Byrskog, Samuel. "Introduction." In *Jesus and Memory: Traditions in Oral and Scribal Perspective*, edited by Werner H. Kelber and Samuel Byrskog, 1–20. Waco: Baylor University Press, 2009.
Cadbury, Henry J. *The Book of Acts in History*. London: A. & C. Black, 1955.
———. "The Knowledge Claimed in Luke's Preface." *Expositor* 8 (1922) 401–20.
———. *The Making of Luke-Acts*. New York: MacMillan, 1927.
———. *The Style and Literary Method of Luke*. Cambridge, MA: Harvard University Press, 1919.
———. *The Treatment of Sources in the Gospel*. Cambridge, MA: Harvard University Press, 1920.
Callaway, P. R. *The History of the Qumran Community: An Investigation*. Journal for the Study of the New Testament: Supplement Series 3. Sheffield: JSOT, 1988.
Campbell, William Sanger. *The We Passages in the Acts of the Apostles: The Narrator as Narrative Character*. Atlanta: Society of Biblical Literature, 2007.
Carter, Warren. "The Disciples." In *Jesus Among Friends and Enemies: A Historical and Literary Introduction to Jesus in the Gospels*, edited by Chris Keith and Larry W. Hurtado, 81–102. Grand Rapids: Baker, 2011.
Casey, Edward S. *Remembering: A Phenomenological Study*. Bloomington: Indiana University Press, 1987.
Cicero. *Rhetorica ad Herennium*. Translated by Harry Caplan. Loeb Classical Library. Cambridge, MA: Harvard University Press, 1954.
Clivaz, Claire. "Rumour: A Category for Articulating the Self-Portraits and Reception of Paul. 'For They Say, "His Letters are Weighty . . . but His Speech is Contemptible' (2 Corinthians 10.10)." In *Paul and the Heritage of Israel: Luke's Narrative Claim upon Paul and Israel's Legacy*, edited by David P. Moessner, et al., 264–81. New York: T. & T. Clark, 2012.
Conzelmann, Hans. *The Theology of St. Luke*. New York: Harper and Row, 1960.
Crossan, John Dominic. *The Birth of Christianity*. San Francisco: HarperSanFrancisco, 1998.
———. *Jesus: A Revolutionary Biography*. San Francisco: HarperCollins, 1994.
———. *Who Killed Jesus? Exposing the Roots of Anti-Semitism in the Gospel Story of the Death of Jesus*. San Fransisco: HarperSanFrancisco, 1995.
Cullmann, Oscar. *Christ and Time*. Translated by Floyd V. Filson. Philadelphia: Westminster, 1945.
———. *Salvation in History*. New York: Harper & Row, 1967.
Dapaah, Daniel S. *The Relationship between John the Baptist and Jesus of Nazareth: A Critical Study*. Lanham, MD: University Press of America, 2005.
Dibelius, Martin. *The Book of Acts: Form, Style, and Theology*. Edited by K. C. Hanson. Minneapolis: Fortress, 2004.
Dilthey, Wilhelm. *Pattern and Meaning in History*. New York: Harper & Row, 1961.
Diodorus Siculus. *Library of History*. Translated by C. H. Oldfather et al. 12 vols. Loeb Classical Library. Cambridge, MA: Harvard University Press, 1933–67.
Dionysius of Halicarnassus. *Critical Essays*. Translated by Stephen Usher. 2 vols. Loeb Classical Library. Cambridge, MA: Harvard University Press, 1985.
———. *Roman Antiquities*. Translated by Earnest Cary. 8 vols. Loeb Classical Library. Cambridge, MA: Harvard University Press, 1937–50.
Dodd, C. H. *The Apostolic Preaching and Its Developments: Three Lectures with an Appendix on Eschatology and History*. New York: Harper, 1936.

Bibliography

Donohue, William A., et al., eds. *Framing Matters: Perspectives on Negotiation Research and Practice in Communication.* New York: Peter Lang, 2011.

Douglas, Mary. "Deciphering a Meal." In *Implicit Meanings: Selected Essays in Anthropology,* 249–75. London: Routledge, 1975.

Dunbabin, Katherine. *The Roman Banquet: Images of Conviviality.* Cambridge: Cambridge University Press, 2003.

Dunn, James D. G. *Baptism in the Holy Spirit: A Re-examination of the New Testament Teaching on the Gift of the Spirit in Relation to Pentecostalism Today.* Naperville, IL: Alec R. Allenson, 1970.

———. *Christianity in the Making.* 2 vols. Grand Rapids: Eerdmans, 2003–9.

Dupont, J. "La question du plan des Actes des Apôtres à la Lumière d'un Texte de Lucien de Samosate." *New Testament Studies* 21 (1974–75) 220–31.

Dupont-Sommer, A. *The Essene Writings from Qumran.* Translated by G. Vermes. Oxford: Blackwell, 1961.

Esler, Philip. *Community and Gospel in Luke-Acts: The Social and Political Motivations of Lucan Theology.* Cambridge: Cambridge University Press, 1987.

Eusebius. *Ecclesiastical History.* Translated by Kirsopp Lake and J. E. L. Oulton. 2 vols. Loeb Classical Library. Cambridge, MA: Harvard University Press, 1926–32.

Evans, Craig A., and James A. Sanders. *Luke and Scripture: The Function of Sacred Tradition in Luke-Acts.* Eugene, OR: Wipf & Stock, 1993.

Fairhurst, Gail T., and Robert A. Sarr. *The Art of Framing: Managing the Language of Leadership.* San Francisco: Jossey-Bass, 1996.

Fearghail, Fearghus O. *The Introduction to Luke-Acts: A Study of the Role of Lk 1,1—4,44 in the Composition of Luke's Two-Volume Work.* AnBib 126. Rome: Pontifical Biblical Institute, 1991.

Flamming, J. "The New Testament Use of Isaiah." *Southwestern Journal of Theology* 11 (1968) 89–103.

Foakes-Jackson, F. J., and Kirsopp Lake, eds. *The Beginnings of Christianity, Part I: The Acts of the Apostles.* 5 vols. London: Macmillan, 1920–33.

Fitzmyer, J. A. *The Acts of the Apostles.* New York: Doubleday, 1998.

Focke, F. "Synkrisis." *Hermes* 58 (1923) 327–68.

Funk, Robert W., and The Jesus Seminar. *The Acts of Jesus: The Search for the Authentic Deeds of Jesus.* San Francisco: HarperSanFrancisco, 1998.

Gamble, Harry Y. *Books and Readers in the Early Church: A History of Early Christian Texts.* New Haven, CT: Yale University Press, 1995.

Gasque, W. Ward. *A History of the Interpretation of the Acts of the Apostles.* Eugene, OR: Wipf & Stock, 2000.

Gerhardsson, Birger. *Memory and Manuscript: Oral Tradition and Written Transmission in Rabbinic Judaism and Early Christianity;* with *Tradition and Transmission in Early Christianity.* Translated by Eric J. Sharpe. Grand Rapids: Eerdmans, 1998.

Goodman, Martin. *Mission and Conversion: Proselytizing in the Religious History of the Roman Empire.* Oxford: Clarendon, 1994.

Green, Joel. *The Gospel of Luke.* The New International Commentary on the New Testament. Grand Rapids: Eerdmans, 1997.

———. *The Theology of the Gospel of Luke.* New Testament Theology. Cambridge: Cambridge University Press, 1995.

Green, Joel, and Michael McKeever. *Luke-Acts and New Testament Historiography.* Grand Rapids: Baker, 1995.

Bibliography

Gregory, Andrew. *The Reception of Luke and Acts in the Period Before Irenaeus: Looking for Luke in the Second Century*. Wissenschafliche Untersuchungen Zum Neuen Testament 2. Tübingen: Mohr Siebeck, 2003.

Gregory, Andrew, and C. Kavin Rowe, eds. *Rethinking the Unity and Reception of Luke and Acts*. Columbia: University of South Carolina Press, 2010.

Grimshaw, James P. *The Matthean Community and the World: An Analysis of Matthew's Food Exchange*. Studies in Biblical Literature 111. New York: Peter Lang, 2008.

Gunkel, Hermann. *Die Wirkungen Des Heilige Geistes*. Gottingen: Vandenhoeck & Ruprecht, 1899.

Haenchen, Ernst. *The Acts of the Apostles*. Philadelphia: Westminster, 1971.

Hahn, Scott W. "Kingdom and Church in Luke-Acts: From Davidic Christology to Kingdom Ecclesiology." In *Reading Luke*, edited by Craig Bartholomew et al., 294-326. Scripture and Hermeneutics 6. Grand Rapids: Zondervan, 2005.

Halbwachs, Maurice. *On Collective Memory*. Translated by Francis J. Ditter Jr. and Vida Yazdi Ditter. New York: Harper & Row, 1980.

Handler, Richard, and Jocelyn Linnekin. "Tradition: Genuine or Spurious." *JAF* 97 (1984) 273-90.

Hanson, K. C., and Douglas E. Oakman. *Palestine in the Time of Jesus: Social Structures and Social Conflicts*. Minneapolis: Fortress, 1998.

Haya-Prats, Gonzalo. *Empowered Believers: The Holy Spirit in the Book of Acts*. Eugene, OR: Wipf & Stock, 2011.

Heath, Malcolm. "Invention." In *Handbook of Classical Rhetoric in the Hellenistic Period, 330 B.C.-A.D. 400*, edited by Stanley Porter, 89-120. Leiden: Brill Academic, 2001.

Hemer, Colin. *The Book of Acts in the Setting of Hellenistic History*. Winona Lake, IN: Eisenbrauns, 1990.

Hengel, M. *The Charismatic Leader and His Followers*. New York: Crossroad, 1981.

Herodotus. *The Persian Wars*. Translated by A. D. Godley. 4 vols. Loeb Classical Library. Cambridge, MA: Harvard University Press, 1920-25.

Hobsbawm, Eric, and Terrence Ranger, eds. *The Invention of Tradition*. Cambridge: Cambridge University Press, 1983.

Hodgson, Peter C. *The Formation of Historical Theology*. Harper and Row, 1966.

Hoehner, H. W. *Herod Antipas*. Society for New Testament Studies Monograph Series 17. Cambridge: Cambridge University Press, 1972.

Houston, George W. *Inside Roman Libraries: Book Collections and Their Management in Antiquity*. Chapel Hill: University of North Carolina Press, 2014.

Hurtado, Larry. *Lord Jesus Christ: Devotion to Jesus in Earliest Christianity*. Grand Rapids: Eerdmans, 2003.

Hutton, Patrick. *History as an Art of Memory*. Burlington: University of Vermont Press, 1993.

Jeremias, J. *New Testament Theology: The Proclamation of Jesus Part 1*. Translated by J. Bowden. London: SCM, 1971.

Jervell, Jacob. *Luke and the People of God: A New Look at Luke-Acts*. Minneapolis: Augsburg, 1972.

Johnson, Luke Timothy. *The Acts of the Apostles*. Sacra Pagina. Collegeville, MN: Liturgical, 1992.

———. *The Gospel of Luke*. Collegeville, MN: Liturgical, 1991.

———. *On Finding the Lukan Community: A Cautious Cautionary Essay*. Missoula, MT: Scholars, 1979.

Bibliography

Josephus. *The Jewish Antiquities*. Translated by H. St. J. Thackeray, et al. 10 vols. Loeb Classical Library. Cambridge, MA: Harvard University Press, 1926–65.

Judge, E. A. "The Social Identity of the First Christians: A Question of Method in Religious History." In *Social Distinctives of the Christians in the First Century: Pivotal Essays by E. A. Judge*, edited by David M. Scholer, 117–36. Peabody, MA: Hendrickson, 2008.

———. "The Social Pattern of the Christian Groups in the First Century." In *Social Distinctives of the Christians in the First Century: Pivotal Essays by E. A. Judge*, edited by David M. Scholer, 1–56. Peabody, MA: Hendrickson, 2008.

Kaye, Bruce N. "Lightfoot and Baur on Earliest Christianity." *Novum Testamentum* 26/3 (1984) 193–224.

Keck, Leander E., and J. Louis Martyn. *Studies in Luke-Acts*. New York: Abingdon, 1966.

Keener, Craig. *Acts: An Exegetical Commentary*. Grand Rapids, Baker, 2012.

———. "First-Person Claims in Some Ancient Historians and Acts." *Journal of Greco-Roman Christianity and Judaism* 10 (2014) 9–23.

———. *The Spirit in the Gospels and Acts*. Peabody, MA: Hendrickson, 1997.

Keith, Chris, and Anthony Le Donne. *Jesus, Criteria, and the Demise of Authenticity*. New York: T. & T. Clark, 2012.

Kennedy, George A. *New Testament Interpretation through Rhetorical Criticism*. Chapel Hill: University of North Carolina Press, 1984.

Kingsbury, Jack Dean. *Conflict in Luke: Jesus, Authorities, Disciples*. Minneapolis: Augsburg, 1991.

Kirk, Alan, and Tom Thatcher, eds. *Memory, Tradition, and Text: Uses of the Past in Early Christianity*. Semeia Studies 52. Atlanta: Society of Biblical Literature, 2005.

Korn, Manfred. *Die Geschichte Jesu in veranderter Zeit: Studien zur bleibenden Bedeutung Jesu im Lukanischen Doppelwerk*. Wissenschaftliche Untersuchungen zum Neuen Testament 2/51. Tübingen: J. C. B. Mohr, 1993.

Kuecker, Aaron. *The Spirit and the "Other": Social Identity, Ethnicity and Intergroup Reconciliation in Luke-Acts*. Library of New Testament Studies. New York: T. & T. Clark, 2011.

Lake, K. "Proselytes and God-Fearers." In *The Beginnings of Christianity, Part I: The Acts of the Apostles*, edited by F. J. Foakes-Jackson and Kirsopp Lake, 5:74–96. London: Macmillan, 1920–33.

Lieu, Judith. *Christian Identity in the Jewish and Greco-Roman World*. Oxford: Oxford University Press, 2004.

Lightfoot, J. B. *The Acts of the Apostles: A Newly Discovered Commentary*. Edited by Ben Witherington III and Todd D. Still. Downers Grove, IL: InterVarsity, 2014.

———. *Galatians*. London: 1865.

Livy. *History of Rome*. Translated by B. O. Foster et al. 10 vols. Loeb Classical Library. Cambridge, MA: Harvard University Press, 1919–2017.

Longenecker, Bruce W. *Rhetoric at the Boundaries: The Art and Theology of New Testament Chain-Link Transition*. Waco: Baylor University Press, 2005.

Longenecker, Richard N. "Taking Up the Cross Daily: Luke-Acts." In *Patterns of Discipleship in the New Testament*, edited by Richard N. Longenecker, 50–76. Grand Rapids: Eerdmans, 1996.

Lowenthal, David. *The Past is a Foreign Country*. New York: Cambridge University Press, 1985.

Lucian. *Lucian*. Translated by K. Kilburn. Loeb Classical Library. Cambridge, MA: Harvard University Press, 1959.

BIBLIOGRAPHY

Lüdemann, G. *Opposition to Paul in Jewish Christianity*. Minneapolis: Fortress, 1989.
Mack, Burton L. *A Myth of Innocence: Mark and Christian Origins*. Philadelphia: Fortress, 1988.
Maddox, R. *The Purpose of Luke-Acts*. Edinburgh: T. & T. Clark, 1982.
Malherbe, A. J. *Social Aspects of Early Christianity*. 2nd ed. Philadelphia: Fortress, 1983.
Malina, Bruce. *The New Testament World: Insights from Cultural Anthropology*. 3rd ed. Louisville: John Knox, 2001.
Malina, Bruce, and Richard L. Rohrbaugh. *Social-Science Commentary on the Synoptic Gospels*. Minneapolis: Fortress, 2003.
Mansfield, M. R. *"Spirit and Gospel" in Mark*. Peabody, MA: Hendrickson, 1987.
Marguerat, Daniel. *The First Christian Historian: Writing the "Acts of the Apostles."* Society for New Testament Studies Monograph Series 121. Cambridge: Cambridge University Press, 2002.
———. "'Paul After Paul': A (Hi)story of Reception." In *Paul and the Heritage of Israel: Paul's Claim upon Israel's Legacy in Luke and Acts in the Light of the Pauline Letters*, edited by David Moessner et al., 70–89. New York: T & T Clark, 2012.
Marincola, John. "Genre, Convention, and Innovation in Greco-Roman Historiography." In *The Limits of Historiography: Genre and Narrative in Ancient Historical Texts*, edited by Christina S. Kraus, 281–324. Leiden: Brill, 1999.
Marshall, I. Howard. *Acts*. Tyndale New Testament Commentaries. Grand Rapids: Eerdmans, 1980.
———. *The Gospel of Luke*. New International Greek Testament Commentary. Grand Rapids: Eerdmans, 1978.
———. *Luke: Historian and Theologian*. 3rd ed. Downers Grove, IL: InterVarsity, 1998.
Martin, Thomas W. "What Makes Glory Glorious? Luke's Account of the Transfiguration Over Against Triumphalism." *Journal for the Study of the New Testament* 29/1 (2006) 3–26.
McCoy, W. J. "In the Shadow of Thucydides." In *History, Literature, and Society in the Book of Acts*, edited by Ben Witherington, 3–31. Cambridge: Cambridge University Press, 1996.
McDonald, Terrence J., ed. *The Historic Turn in the Human Sciences*. Ann Arbor: University of Michigan Press, 1996.
McGing, Brian. *Polybius' Histories*. Oxford: Oxford University Press, 2010.
McKnight, Scot. "Jesus and the Twelve." In *Key Events in the Life of the Historical Jesus*, edited by Darrell L. Bock and Robert L. Webb, 181–214. Grand Rapids: Eerdmans, 2009.
———. *A Light Among the Gentiles: Jewish Missionary Activity in the Second Temple Period*. Minneapolis: Fortress, 1991.
Meier, J. P. "The Circle of the Twelve: Did It Exist During Jesus' Ministry?" *Journal of Biblical Literature* 116 (1997) 635–72.
———. "John the Baptist in Matthew's Gospel." *Journal of Biblical Literature* 99 (1980) 383–405.
———. *A Marginal Jew: Rethinking the Historical Jesus*. 4 vols. New York: Doubleday, 1991–2009.
Menzies, Robert P. *The Development of Early Christian Pneumatology with Special Reference to Luke-Acts*. Journal for the Study of the New Testament Supplement Series 54. Sheffield: Sheffield, 1991.
———. "Luke and the Spirit: A Reply to James Dunn." *JPT* 4 (1994) 115–38.

BIBLIOGRAPHY

Meyer, Eduard. *Ursprung und Anfänge des Christentums*. Berlin, 1921.
Minear, Paul. "Luke's Use of the Birth Stories." In *Studies in Luke-Acts*, edited by Leander E. Keck and J. Louis Martyn, 111–30. Nashville: Abingdon, 1966.
Moessner, David P. "The Appeal and Power of Poetics (Luke 1:1-4)." In *Jesus and the Heritage of Israel: Luke's Narrative Claim upon Israel's Legacy*, edited by David P. Moessner, 84–126. Harrisburg, PA: Trinity, 1999.
———. *Jesus and the Heritage of Israel: Luke's Narrative Claim upon Israel's Legacy*. Harrisburg, PA: Trinity, 1999.
———. *Lord of the Banquet: The Literary and Theological Significance of the Lukan Travel Narrative*. Harrisburg, PA: Trinity, 1989.
———. "Mediator, Miracle-Worker, Doctor of the Church? The Continuing Mystery of Paul in the New Testament and in Early Christianity." In *Paul and the Heritage of Israel: Paul's Claim upon Israel's Legacy in Luke and Acts in the Light of the Pauline Letters*, edited by David Moessner et al., 318–23. New York: T. & T. Clark, 2012.
———, et al., eds., *Paul and the Heritage of Israel: Paul's Claim upon Israel's Legacy in Luke and Acts in the Light of the Pauline Letters*. New York: T. & T. Clark, 2012.
———. "The 'Script' of the Scriptures in Acts: Suffering as God's 'Plan' (Βουλή) for the World for the 'Release of Sins.'" In *History, Literature, and Society in the Book of Acts*, edited by Ben Witherington III, 218–50. Cambridge: Cambridge University Press, 1996.
———. "The Triadic Synergy of Hellenistic Poetics in the Narrative Epistemology of Dionysius of Halicarnassus and the Authorial Intent of the Evangelist Luke (Luke 1:1-4; Acts 1:1-8)." *Neotestamenica* 42/2 (2008) 289–303.
Muller, C., ed. *Geographi Graeci Minores I*. Paris: Didot, 1855.
Murray, Michele. *Playing a Jewish Game: Gentile Christian Judaizing in the First and Second Centuries CE*. Waterloo, ON: Wilfrid Laurier University Press, 2004.
Neill, Stephen, and Tom Wright. *The Interpretation of the New Testament: 1861–1961*. Oxford: Oxford University Press, 1964.
Neyrey, Jerome. "The Forensic Defense Speech and Paul's Trial Speeches in Acts 22-26: Form and Function." In *Luke-Acts: New Perspectives from the Society of Biblical Literature Seminar*, edited by C. H. Talbert, 210–24. New York: Crossroads, 1984.
Nolland, John. *Luke*. 3 vols. Word Biblical Commentary 35 A-C. Dallas: Word, 1989–93.
Olick, Jeffrey K., and Daniel Levy. "Collective Memory and Cultural Constraint: Holocaust Myth and Rationality in German Politics." *ASR* 62 (1997) 921–36.
———, et al., eds. *The Collective Memory Reader*. Oxford: Oxford University Press, 2011.
Oliver, H. H. "The Lucan Birth Stories and the Purpose of Luke-Acts." *NTS* 10 (1963–64) 202–26.
Ong, W. *Interfaces of the Word: Studies in the Evolution of Consciousness and Culture*. Ithaca, NY: Cornell University Press, 1977.
———. *Orality and Literacy: The Technologizing of the Word*. London: Methuen, 1982.
O'Toole, Robert F. "Luke's Message in Luke 9:1–50." *Catholic Biblical Quarterly* 49 (1987) 80–95.
Ovid. *Fasti*. Translated by James G. Frazer. Cambridge, MA: Harvard University Press, 1931.
Painter, J. "Christology and the Fourth Gospel." *AusBR* 31 (1983) 45–62.
Parsons, Mikeal. *Acts*. Paideia. Grand Rapids: Baker Academic, 2008.
———. *The Departure of Jesus: The Ascension Narratives in Context*. Sheffield: Sheffield Academic, 1987.

Bibliography

———. *Luke: Storyteller, Interpreter, Evangelist*. Peabody, MA: Hendrickson, 2007.
Parsons, Mikeal, and M. M. Culy. *Acts: A Handbook on the Greek Text*. Waco: Baylor University Press, 2003.
Parsons, Mikeal, and Richard Pervo. *Rethinking the Unity of Luke and Acts*. Minneapolis: Fortress, 1990.
Paranuk, H. van Dyke. "Transitional Techniques in the Bible." *Journal of Biblical Literature* 102 (1983) 525-48.
Penner, Todd. *In Praise of Christian Origins: Stephen and the Hellenists in Lukan Apologetic Historiography*. New York: T. & T. Clark, 2004.
Pervo, Richard I. *Profit with Delight: The Literary Genre of the Acts of the Apostles*. Philadelphia: Fortress, 1987.
Phillips, Kendall R., ed. *Framing Public Memory*. Tuscaloosa: The University of Alabama Press, 2004.
Philo. *On the Decalogue. On the Special Laws, Books 1-3*. Translated by F. H. Colson. Loeb Classical Library 320. Cambridge, MA: Harvard University Press, 1937.
———. *On the Special Laws, Book 4. On the Virtues. On Rewards and Punishments*. Translated by F. H. Colson. Loeb Classical Library 341. Cambridge, MA: Harvard University Press, 1939.
Philostratus. *Life of Apollonius of Tyana*. Translated by Christopher P. Jones. Loeb Classical Library. 2 vols. Cambridge, MA: Harvard University Press, 2005.
Plato. *Euthyphro. Apology. Crito. Phaedo. Phaedrus*. Translated by Harold North Fowler. Loeb Classical Library. Cambridge, MA: Harvard University Press, 1914.
Plümacher, Eckhard. *Lukas als hellenistischer Schriftsteller: Studien zur Apostelgeschichte*. Göttingen: Vandenhoeck & Ruprecht, 1972.
———. "The Mission Speeches in Acts and Dionysius of Halicarnassus." In *Jesus and the Heritage of Israel: Luke's Narrative Claim upon Israel's Legacy*, edited by David P. Moessner, 251-66. Harrisburg, PA: Trinity, 1999.
Plutarch. *Lives*. Translated by Bernadotte Perrin. 11 vols. Loeb Classical Library. Cambridge, MA: Harvard University Press, 1914-26.
Polybius. *Histories*. Translated by W. R. Paton. 6 vols. Loeb Classical Library. Cambridge, MA: Harvard University Press, 1922-27.
Porter, Stanley E., ed. *Handbook of Classical Rhetoric in the Hellenistic Period, 330 B.C.-A.D. 400*. Leiden: Brill Academic, 2001.
———. *The Paul of Acts: Essays in Literary Criticism, Rhetoric, and Theology*. Wissenschaftliche Untersuchungen zum Neuen Testament 115. Tubingen: Mohr, 1999.
———. "The Theoretical Justification for Application of Rhetorical Categories to Pauline Epistolary Literature." In *Rhetoric and the New Testament*, edited by S. E. Porter and T. H. Olbricht, 100-122. Sheffield: Sheffield Academic, 1993.
Quintilian. *Institutio oratorio*. Translated by H. E. Butler. Loeb Classical Library. Cambridge, MA: Harvard University Press, 1986.
Rabinowitz, Peter. "Truth in Fiction: A Reexamination of Audiences." *Critical Inquiry* 4 (1977) 121-41.
Rebenich, Stefan. "Historical Prose." In *Handbook of Classical Rhetoric in the Hellenistic Period, 330 B.C.-A.D. 400*, edited by Stanley E. Porter, 265-338. Leiden: Brill Academic, 2001.
Rickman, H. P. Introduction to *Pattern and Meaning in History*, by Wilhelm Dilthey. New York: Harper & Row, 1961.

Bibliography

Ricoeur, Paul. *Memory, History, Forgetting*. Translated by Kathleen Blamey and David Pellauer. Chicago: University of Chicago, 2004.

———. *Time and Narrative*. Translated by Kathleen McLaughlin and David Pellauer. 3 vols. Chicago: University of Chicago, 1990.

Robbins, Vernon K. "The Claims of the Prologues and Greco-Roman Rhetoric: The Prefaces to Luke and Acts in Light of Greco-Roman Rhetorical Strategies." In *Jesus and the Heritage of Israel: Luke's Narrative Claim upon Israel's Legacy*, edited by David P. Moessner, 63–83. Harrisburg, PA: Trinity, 1999.

———. *Exploring the Texture of Texts: A Guide to Socio-Rhetorical Interpretation*. Valley Forge, PA: Trinity, 1996.

———. "Luke-Acts: A Mixed Population Seeks a Home in the Roman Empire." In *Images of Empire*, edited by Loveday Alexander, 202–21. Journal for the Study of the Old Testament Supplement Series 122. Sheffield: Sheffield Academic Press, 1991.

Rodriguez, Rafael. *Structuring Early Christian Memory: Jesus in Tradition Performance and Text*. New York: T. & T. Clark, 2010.

Roloff, J. "'Die Paulus-Darstellung des Lukas': Ihre geschichtlichen Voraussetzungen und ihr theologisches Ziel." *EvTh* 39 (1979) 510–31.

Rothschild, Clare K. *Luke-Acts and the Rhetoric of History: An Investigation of Early Christian Historiography*. Wissenschaftliche Untersuchungen zum Neuen Testament 175. Tübingen: Mohr Siebeck, 2004.

Sanders, E. P. *Jesus and Judaism*. Philadelphia: Fortress, 1985.

Satterthwaite, Philip E. "Acts Against the Background of Classical Rhetoric." In *The Book of Acts in Its Ancient Literary Setting*, edited by Bruce W. Winter, 337–79. Grand Rapids: Eerdmans, 1993.

Schmidt, K. L. *Der Rahmen der Geschichte Jesu*. Berlin, 1919.

Schmithals, Walter. *Paul and the Gnostics*. Translated by John E. Steely. Nashville: Abingdon, 1972.

Schnabel, Eckhard. *Acts*. Zondervan Exegetical Commentary on the New Testament. Grand Rapids: Zondervan, 2012.

———. *Early Christian Mission*. 2 vols. Downers Grove, IL: InterVarsity, 2004.

Schneemelcher, Wilhelm, and R. McL. Wilson, eds. *New Testament Apocrypha*. 2 vols. Tübingen: J. C. B. Mohr, 1990.

Schubert, P. "The Structure and Significance of Luke 24." In *Neutestamentliche Studien für Rudolf Bultmann*, edited by W. Eltester, 165–86. Berlin: Töpelmann, 1954.

Schudson, Michael. *Watergate in American Memory: How We Remember, Forget, and Reconstruct the Past*. New York: Basic, 1992.

Schwartz, Barry. *Abraham Lincoln and the Forge of National Memory*. Chicago: University of Chicago Press, 2000.

———. "Memory as a Cultural System: Abraham Lincoln in World War II." *ASR* 61 (1996) 908–27.

———. "The Social Context of Commemoration: A Study in Collective Memory." *Social Forces* 61 (1982) 374–402.

Schweitzer, Albert. *The Quest of the Historical Jesus*. Translated by W. Montgomery. Mineola, NY: Dover, 2005.

Seters, Jon van. *In Search of History: Historiography in the Ancient World and the Origins of Biblical History*. New Haven, CT: Yale University Press, 1983.

Shiell, William D. *Delivering from Memory: The Effect of Performance on the Early Christian Audience*. Eugene, OR: Pickwick, 2011.

Shiner, Whitney. *Proclaiming the Gospel: First-Century Performance of Mark.* Harrisburg, PA: Trinity, 2003.
Simons, Robert C. "Rhetoric and Luke 1–2: A Rhetorical Study of an Extended Narrative Passage." PhD diss., Trinity College Bristol, 2006.
Smith, Dennis E. *From Symposium to Eucharist: The Banquet in the Early Christian World.* Minneapolis: Augsburg Fortress, 2003.
———. "Table Fellowship as a Literary Motif in the Gospel of Luke." *Journal of Biblical Literature* 106 (1987) 613–38.
Smith, Dennis E., and Hal Taussig, eds. *Meals in the Early Christian World: Social Formation, Experimentation, and Conflict at the Table.* New York: Palgrave Macmillan, 2012.
Soards, Marion L. *The Speeches in Acts: Their Content, Context, and Concerns.* Louisville: Westminster John Knox, 1994.
Songer, Y. H. "Isaiah and the New Testament." *RevExp* 65 (1968) 459–70.
Spencer, F. S. "Acts and Modern Literary Approaches." In *The Book of Acts in Its Ancient Literary Setting*, edited by Bruce W. Winter, 381–414. Grand Rapids: Eerdmans, 1993.
Squires, John T. *The Plan of God in Luke-Acts.* Cambridge: Cambridge University Press, 1993.
Stanton, Graham N. "The Spirit in the Writings of Justin Martyr." In *The Holy Spirit and Christian Origins*, edited by Graham N. Stanton et al., 321–24. Grand Rapids: Eerdmans, 2004.
Stanton, Graham N., et al., eds. *The Holy Spirit and Christian Origins: Essays in Honor of James D. G. Dunn.* Grand Rapids: Eerdmans, 2004.
Sterling, Gregory E. "From the 'Least of All the Saints' to the 'Apostle of Jesus Christ': The Transformation of Paul in the First Century." In *Paul and the Heritage of Israel: Paul's Claim upon Israel's Legacy in Luke and Acts in the Light of the Pauline Letters*, edited by David Moessner et al., 220–44. New York: T. & T. Clark, 2012.
———. *Historiography and Self-Definition: Josephos, Luke-Acts, and Apologetic Historiography.* Leiden: Brill, 1992.
Stuckenbruck, Loren T. "The Holy Spirit in the Ascension of Isaiah." In *The Holy Spirit and Christian Origins: Essays in Honor of James D. G. Dunn*, edited by Graham N. Stanton et al., 308–20. Grand Rapids: Eerdmans, 2004.
Stylianou, P. J. *A Historical Commentary on Diodorus Siculus, Book 15.* Oxford: Oxford University Press, 1998.
Sukenik, E. L. *The Dead Sea Scrolls of the Hebrew University.* Edited by N. Avigad. Jerusalem: Magnes, 1955.
Sumney, Jerry. *Identifying Paul's Opponents: The Question of Method in 2 Corinthians.* New York: Bloomsbury, 2015.
Tacitus. *Agricola. Germania. Dialogue on Oratory.* Translated by M. Hutton and W. Peterson. Loeb Classical Library. Cambridge: Cambridge University Press, 1914.
Talbert, Charles. *Literary Patterns, Theological Themes, and the Genre of Luke-Acts.* Missoula, MT: Scholars, 1974.
———. "The Lukan Presentation of Jesus' Ministry in Galilee." *Rev Exp* 64 (1967) 492–97.
———. "Prophecies of Future Greatness: The Contribution of Greco-Roman Biographies to an Understanding of Luke 1:5—4:15." In *The Divine Helmsman: Studies on God's Control of Human Events, Presented to Lou H. Silberman*, edited by James L. Crenshaw and Samuel Sandmel, 129–41. New York: Ktav, 1980.

Bibliography

———. *Reading Luke: A Literary and Theological Commentary on the Third Gospel*. Macon, GA: Smyth & Helwys, 2002.

———. *Reading Luke-Acts in Its Mediterranean Milieu*. Supplements to Novum Testamentum. Leiden: Brill, 2003.

Tannehill, Robert. *The Narrative Unity of Luke-Acts: A Literary Interpretation*. 2 vols. Minneapolis: Fortress, 1986, 1990.

———. *The Shape of Luke's Story: Essays on Luke-Acts*. Eugene, OR: Cascade, 2005.

Taussig, Hal. *In the Beginning was the Meal: Social Experimentation and Early Christian Identity*. Minneapolis: Fortress, 2009.

Taylor, Joan E. *The Immerser: John the Baptist with Second Temple Judaism*. Grand Rapids: Eerdmans, 1997.

Taylor, R. O. P. *Groundwork for the Gospels, With Some Collected Papers*. Oxford: Blackwell, 1946.

Tellbe, Mikael. "The Prototypical Christ-believer: Early Christian Identity Formation in Ephesus." In *Exploring Early Christian Identity*, edited by Bengt Holmberg, 115–38. Wissenschaftliche Untersuchungen zum Neuen Testament 226. Tübingen: Mohr Siebeck, 2008.

Thatcher, Tom. *Why John Wrote a Gospel: Jesus—Memory—History*. Louisville: Westminster John Knox, 2006.

Thucydides. *History of the Peloponnesian War*. Translated by C. F. Smith. 4 vols. Loeb Classical Library. Cambridge, MA: Harvard University Press, 1919–23.

Tite, P. L. *Compositional Transitions in 1 Peter: An Analysis of the Letter-Opening*. London: International Scholars 1997.

Tosh, John. *The Pursuit of History: Aims, Methods and New Directions in the Study of History*. New York: Routledge, 2015.

Trebilco, Paul. *The Early Christians in Ephesus From Paul to Ignatius*. Tübingen: Mohr Siebeck, 2004.

Trocme, E. *Le "Livre des Acts" et L'Histoire*. Paris: University of France Press, 1957.

Trompf, G. W. *The Idea of Historical Recurrence in Western Thought: From Antiquity to the Reformation*. Berkley: University of California Press, 1979.

Turner, Max. *Power from on High: The Spirit in Israel's Restoration and Witness in Luke-Acts*. Journal of Pentecostal Theology Supplement 9. New York: T. & T. Clark, 1996.

———. "The Significance of Receiving the Spirit in Luke-Acts: A Survey of Modern Scholarship." *Trinity Journal* 2 (1981) 131–58.

Tyson, Joseph B. "The Birth Narratives and the Beginning of Luke's Gospel." *Semeia* 52 (1991) 103–20.

———. *Images of Judaism in Luke-Acts*. Columbia: University of South Carolina Press, 2010.

Unnik, W. C. van. "Once More St. Luke's Prologue." *Neotestamentica* 7 (1973) 7–26.

———. "Remarks on the Purpose of Luke's Historical Writing." In *Sparsa Collecta: The Collected Essays of W. C. van Unnik*, 1:6–15. Supplements to Novum Testamentum 29. Leiden: Brill, 1973.

Vielhauer, Philipp. "On the 'Paulinism' of Acts." In *Studies in Luke-Acts*, edited by L. E. Keck and J. L. Martyn, 33–50. Nashville: Abingdon, 1966.

Völkel, Martin. "Exegetische Erwägungen zum Verständnis des Begriffs im lukanischen Prolog." *New Testament Studies* 20 (1973–74) 289–99.

Vos, J. S. *Traditionsgeschichtliche Untersuchungen zur paulinischen Pneumatologie*. Assen: Van Gorcum, 1973.

BIBLIOGRAPHY

Walaskay, Paul W. *"And so we came to Rome": The Political Perspective of St. Luke.* Society for New Testament Studies Monograph Series 49. Cambridge: Cambridge University Press, 2005.

Watson, D. F. "Paul's Speech to the Ephesian Elders (Acts 20.17-38): Epideictic Rhetoric of Farewell." In *Persuasive Artistry: Studies in New Testament Rhetoric in Honor of George A. Kennedy*, edited by D. B. Watson, 184-208. Journal for the Study of the New Testament: Supplement Series 50. Sheffield: Sheffield Academic Press, 1990.

Webb, Robert L. *John the Baptizer and Prophet: A Sociohistorical Study.* Eugene, OR: Wipf & Stock, 2006.

Wenk, Matthias. *Community-Forming Power: The Socio-Ethical Role of the Spirit in Luke-Acts.* New York: T. & T. Clark, 2000.

Wilcox, M. "The God-Fearers in Acts—A Reconsideration." *Journal for the Study of the New Testament* 13 (1981) 102-22.

Will, Edouard, and Claude Orrieux. *Proselytisme juif? Histoire d'une erreur.* Paris: Les Belles Lettres, 1992.

Wilson, Stephen G. *The Gentiles and the Gentile Mission in Luke-Acts.* Cambridge: Cambridge University Press, 1973.

Wink, Walter. *John the Baptist in the Gospel Tradition.* Society for New Testament Studies Monograph Series 7. Cambridge: Cambridge University Press, 1968.

Winter, Bruce W., ed. *The Book of Acts in Its First Century Setting.* 5 vols. Grand Rapids: Eerdmans, 1993-96.

Witherington, Ben, III. *The Acts of the Apostles: A Socio-Rhetorical Commentary.* Grand Rapids: Eerdmans, 1998.

———. *Jesus, Paul, and the End of the World.* Downers Grove, IL: InterVarsity, 1992.

———. *Letters and Homilies for Hellenized Christians: A Socio-Rhetorical Commentary on Titus, 1-2 Timothy and 1-3 John.* Downers Grove, IL: InterVarsity, 2006.

———. *The Letters to Philemon, the Colossians, and the Ephesians: A Socio-Rhetorical Commentary on the Captivity Epistles.* Grand Rapids: Eerdmans, 2007.

———. *New Testament Rhetoric: An Introductory Guide to the Art of Persuasion in and of the New Testament.* Eugene, OR: Wipf & Stock, 2009.

———. *Women in the Ministry of Jesus: A Study of Jesus' Attitudes to Women and Their Roles as Reflected in His Earthly Life.* New York: Cambridge University Press, 1984.

———, ed. *History, Literature, and Society in the Book of Acts.* Cambridge: Cambridge University Press, 1996.

Wolter, Michael. "The Development of Pauline Christianity From a 'Religion of Conversion' to a 'Religion of Tradition.'" In *Paul and the Heritage of Israel: Paul's Claim upon Israel's Legacy in Luke and Acts in the Light of the Pauline Letters*, edited by David Moessner et al., 50-69. New York: T. & T. Clark, 2012.

———. *Die Pastoralbriefe als Paulustradition.* Forschungen zur Religion und Literatur des Alten und Neuen Testaments 146. Gottingen: Vandenhoeck & Ruprecht, 1988.

Wright, N. T. *Jesus and the Victory of God.* Minneapolis: Fortress, 1997.

———. *The New Testament and the People of God.* Minneapolis: Fortress, 1992.

———. *The Resurrection of the Son of God.* Minneapolis: Fortress, 2003.

Wuellner, Wilhelm. "Arrangement." In *Handbook of Classical Rhetoric in the Hellenistic Period, 330 B.C.-A.D. 400*, edited by Stanley Porter, 51-88. Leiden: Brill Academic, 2001.

Yerushalmi, Yosef Hayim. *Zakhor: Jewish History and Jewish Memory.* Seattle: University of Washington Press, 1982.

Bibliography

Zerubavel, Eviatar. *Time Maps: Collective Memory and the Social Shape of the Past.* Chicago: The University of Chicago Press, 2003.

Zerubavel, Yael. *Recovered Roots: Collective Memory and the Making of Israeli National Tradition.* Chicago: The University of Chicago Press, 1995.

www.ingramcontent.com/pod-product-compliance
Lightning Source LLC
Chambersburg PA
CBHW051942160426
43198CB00013B/2265